Life's Too Short
to Fold Your
Underwear

Life's Too Short to Fold your Underwear

Real-Life Wit and Wisdom
to Help You Sort Out
What Matters Most

Patricia Lorenz

Guideposts
New York, New York

Life's Too Short to Fold Your Underwear

ISBN-13: 978-0-8249-4719-4
ISBN-10: 0-8249-4719-3

Published by Guideposts
16 East 34th Street
New York, New York 10016
www.guideposts.com

Distributed by Ideals Publications, a Guideposts company
2636 Elm Hill Pike, Suite 120
Nashville, Tennessee 37214

Guideposts and *Ideals* are registered trademarks of Guideposts.

Acknowledgments
Every attempt has been made to credit the sources of copyrighted material used in this book. If any such acknowledgment has been inadvertently omitted or miscredited, receipt of such information would be appreciated.

Scripture quotations marked (KJV) are taken from *The King James Version of the Bible.*

Scripture quotations marked (RSV) are taken from the *Revised Standard Version of the Bible.* Copyright © 1946, 1952, 1971 by Division of Christian Education of the National Council of Churches of Christ in the U.S.A. Used by permission.

Scripture quotations marked (TLB) are taken from *The Living Bible.* Copyright © 1971 by Tyndale House Publishers, Wheaton, IL 60187. All rights reserved.

"Invitation" is from *Where the Sidewalk Ends* by Shel Silverstein. Copyright © 1974 by Evil Eye Music, Inc. Used by permission of HarperCollins Publishers.

Lyrics from "The Bug" are from the album *Golden Live* by Mark Knopfler. Copyright © 1996 by Mark Knopfler. All rights reserved.

Library of Congress Cataloging-in-Publication Data

Lorenz, Patricia.
    Life's too short to fold your underwear : real-life wit and wisdom to help you sort out what matters most / by Patricia Lorenz.
        p. cm.
    Originally published: Carmel, N.Y. : Guideposts, c2004.
    ISBN-13: 978-0-8249-4719-4
    1. Conduct of life. 2. Life—Humor. I. Title.
    BJ1581.2.L685 2007
    242.02'07—dc22
                                    2006024324

Edited by Stephanie Castillo Samoy
Cover art by B. K. Taylor
Designed by Marisa Jackson

Printed and bound in the United States of America

10 9 8 7 6 5

Thank you . . .

To my four children Jeanne, Julia, Michael and Andrew, their spouses, my grandchildren, brother, sister and their families, and my dad Ed Kobbeman, stepmom Bev, and all my dear friends, for filling my life with enough experiences and grand adventures to fill yet another whole book. You have all made the journey an incredible ride for me.

To all the talented, hard-working people at Guideposts in New York City.

To Stephanie Castillo Samoy, my gifted, patient and oh-so-helpful editor at Guideposts. Bless you for all your work on this project.

To all the people I wrote about in this book. Your inspiration is what keeps me knowing for sure what's important and what isn't in this life.

—Patricia Lorenz

Contents

Introduction

IT'S TRUE. I *don't* fold my underwear. Ever. I just open the underwear drawers and toss it all in. It's fun. It's freeing. It's a time-saver. Who's going to know? Don't we all have better things to do with our time than fold underwear?

Most of us have things we don't do for lots of different reasons. One woman I know says life's too short to sort silverware so she just tosses all the knives, forks and spoons in the drawer unsorted. If it works for her, why not?

Another friend says life's too short to match your socks, set your hair or play around with makeup. Of course we're talking about a woman with naturally wavy hair and flawless skin, a woman who doesn't need to set her hair or wear makeup. But I still like her attitude.

A forty-something man who started his own business says life's too short to dedicate yourself to corporate America. Attaboy! I left corporate America in 1992 to stay home and write full-time. Even though corporate America pays more, I wouldn't trade this life for anything.

Another friend has a whole list of "life's too short for . . ." things. She says life's too short to bike uphill, age wine or whine about age, wait in line, paint your toenails, make a short story long, or listen to gossip. To all those I say,

"Go, girl!" Thanks to her inspiration I'm now looking for a place where all the hills are going down.

This book is not just about things that are a waste of time. This book is about striving for common sense in a world that's sometimes whacked-out. It's about what to do when our priorities get screwed up, rearranged, ignored or set aside.

This book contains my own personal essays and true stories about life, some humorous, others serious. Everything from what I learned when my dad won the outhouse race to how a single parent of four with a below-poverty income gets her kids through college and then proceeds to lead the good life. From the foibles of fund-raising to getting rid of clutter and avoiding overload by having one big fit.

This book also contains stories I wrote about other people who have an interesting outlook on life . . . people who experience life-changing events and who have the sense to let those experiences make their lives and relationships more fulfilling and happier. Stories so powerful they can motivate the rest of us to change the way we look at life and at the world.

I think life's too short to do a number of things we do and I've covered many of them in this book. I hope it will help you take a look at your own priorities. So instead of folding your underwear or obsessing about being in complete control of everyone's everything, my wish for you is that my stories will calm you, inspire you to make some changes in your life and give you a sense of what living joyfully is all about. As you read, I hope you laugh and cry, but most of all, may these stories give you wings to become a person who truly knows what's important in life and what isn't.

Chapter One

Family Foibles and Frolics

Families. Don't you just love 'em? Life within a family is often like getting caught in the spin cycle of the washing machine. It's no wonder when people are asked to sum up their past week in one word that most people in America say "stressful" or "hectic." It's true. They did surveys and really asked that question to thousands of people. Maybe hundreds of thousands. Don't ask who "they" is. I'm not a crazed fact-checker. I'm just a member of a family who finds stuff like that pretty interesting. I also think it's important that we take a step back and try to figure out how to de-stress our lives while at the same time understanding that family is the single most important element in our lives. And when it comes down to it, life's too short not to cherish your family every single day . . . in spite of, or maybe because of, all their foibles and frolics.

Life's Too Short to Dance with Disaster

RUNNING A HOUSEHOLD with a pack of kids does have its moments. One time one of those moments lasted a full eight hours. It all started with a one-hundred-dollar trip to the grocery store, a broken jar of jelly, three neighbors who dropped in at 10:00 AM for tea, a missed doctor's appointment, and an Avon lady who talked about my sagging chin and crow's feet.

By 3:00 PM the day was just getting started. Then there were the four kids and their eight friends who tracked mud all over the house, the fifteen phone calls (all for the kids), one phone call for me from a guy desperate to sell me a new roof, the bag of unpopped popcorn that split and tumbled out of the cupboard and into the innards of the gas stove, and the roller skate at the front door that I tripped over and skinned my shin.

But the event that did me in, tempting me to turn in my motherhood button once and for all, came while I was fixing supper. I told the two-year-old to go down to the family room and turn off the TV. *Sesame Street* was over and Andrew had come upstairs insisting that he help fix supper. Believe me, a tired, harried parent doesn't need help from a two-year-old at that time of day.

I knew Andrew could follow simple directions. So I said very clearly and slowly, "Honey, go downstairs and push the button on the TV and turn off the TV." I repeated it three times, emphasizing the words, *push, off* and *TV*. I knew he'd figure it out. He knew where the *off* button was. After all, he took delight in pushing it every night during the climax of every movie we watched.

So downstairs he went, to do a nice deed for Mommy. I went back to the sink to wash the carrots and trim the broccoli. Then it happened. The loudest crash the walls in our house had ever heard. I was so startled I couldn't move. I kept waiting for Andrew to scream. But the silence was more frightening than the crash.

I restarted my heart and raced down the steps, half expecting to find Andrew lying unconscious amidst shattered patio doors. I blurted out a fast prayer. Then I stopped cold.

He was standing there *behind* the TV stand, smiling a banana-sized grin that said, "Aren't you proud of me, Mommy?" That smile just kept radiating across his whole face as he said, "Andrew pushed off the TV!"

There was the color TV set face down on the floor. Two of the knobs were broken off. The screen was smashed. The plants I'd watered that morning that used to sit on top of the set were oozing mud and goo into the carpet. Broken plants and ceramic pots were spread all over the room.

And there was Andrew smiling, proud as a panda, because he had done just what Mommy asked. He'd pushed off the TV. Boy, did he.

I pulled him into my arms and sat on the couch rocking him back and forth. I thanked God that he wasn't hurt. I prayed for patience. I prayed that I wouldn't take up child abuse for a hobby. I prayed that this day would end quickly.

That's when my best friend rang the doorbell and walked inside. By the time I got upstairs she was pouring water into the teapot and had crushed a few more popcorn kernels into the new linoleum floor. She asked in her *since-you-only-work-part-time-and-today-was-your-day-off* envious voice, "Well, what did you do to keep busy today, lady of leisure?"

Somehow, I don't think she'll ever ask that question again.

Life's Too Short to Deliver Papers

WHEN I WAS A CHILD I listened to the stories about how my grandparents walked ten miles to school and then went home to work five hours on the farm. From my parents I heard all about the Depression and how far a nickel had to go in those days.

It worked. I became a frugal soul—and a lifeguard, babysitter, grocery checker and typist—to pay for college.

I encouraged my own offspring to babysit, mow lawns, rake leaves, shovel snow and take care of pets for pay, in addition to working at various fast-food, drug and clothing stores to make money for college.

When my fourteen-year-old daughter told me she had a chance to take over a friend's paper route for a week while the friend was on vacation, my eyes lit up with dollar signs, especially after she said she could earn twenty-five dollars in one week.

"How many papers?" I asked. "Do you have the route list? How long will it take?"

My young entrepreneur assured me that her one-week-only newspaper delivery route would be a breeze. "I'll get up at five AM and be home by seven. Then I can get ready for school."

"Five AM?" I squeaked. "You mean people actually get up at five AM?"

"Well, I don't know about others, but paper girls do." She sounded so confident.

Luckily, her first route day was on a Saturday. I heard her stumble around the kitchen in the middle of the night, then go outside and come back moments later. It sounded like she was dragging a body across the floor. It must have been the newspapers.

Soon she was out the door with a bright yellow canvas newspaper bag slung over her back. Two and a half hours later she returned—exhausted, her cheeks aglow from the freezing cold Wisconsin morning.

I looked at the clock. "At this rate you're going to have to get up about four-fifteen AM in order to have enough time to eat breakfast and get ready for school," I said. "No way! Honey, you need more sleep than that."

"I can do it, Mom," she said. "I'll go to bed at nine every night. It's good exercise. I like getting up early. Besides, I'm going to earn twenty-five dollars!"

Before my brain was engaged I interrupted with, "Well, instead of taking my daily walk at eight AM, I suppose I could get up at five and deliver half the route for you."

"Hey, that'd be great!" she said. "I'd still have time to practice piano in the mornings." She knew the way to my heart.

Monday, 5:00 AM crashed into my consciousness with the gentleness of a Marine sergeant driving a tank over my body as the alarm clock went off. After slapping the clock, I almost rolled over and went back to sleep. It was the middle of the night, for heaven's sake! Then I remembered the paper route. Oh yes. Get up. Get dressed. Deliver papers. Come home. I can handle it.

I pulled my jogging suit over my long underwear. The radio said the temperature was in the low twenties. Next I pulled on heavy wool socks, boots, ski jacket, scarf, cap and gloves. I was ready to tackle the newspaper business.

I already had made a list of the house numbers that I was responsible for. I put the list in my pocket, grabbed what seemed like a three-hundred-pound stack of newspapers, jammed them into my favorite oversized straw beach basket and opened the front door.

Whoa! This couldn't be morning! It was black as coal out there. And cold! After that first breath of 5:00 AM oxygen I was more awake than I am most days after being up three hours.

I walked a block to the start of my route and waved to my daughter, who turned left where I turned right. As I surveyed the block ahead of me, my spirits perked up. It was a whole street of look-alike double condominiums. All the mailboxes and round newspaper tubes were along the street in nice neat rows.

I checked my list. First house, paper in the tube. Second house, paper in the tube. Third house, skip. Fourth house, paper in the tube. Fifth, sixth, seventh, eighth houses, skip. "What? These people don't read?" I grumbled to myself.

Ninth house, paper in the door. *What? I have to walk clear up to the house and put the paper inside the storm door? Don't they know how much fun it is to go out to the street at 6:00 AM in the freezing cold in your bathrobe and slippers to get the paper? They're going to make me walk all the way up to the front door? The nerve!*

Next stop, the house with the dog. The minute I opened the storm door to throw in the paper, a dog barked an ear-piercing warning to the inhabitants. *It's only me, dog*, I thought. *The sweet, lovable paper lady. Chill out, and go back to sleep.*

Around the bend, house after house. A garage door rolled up and a man drove his car down the driveway. *Wow, another human being out at this time of day.* I smiled and waved to the guy.

"Hey, buddy, wanna toss me the paper?"

"I'm not your buddy. I'm a thirty-seven-year-old mother of four who's working her way through college."

"*Huh? Sure*, lady." He drove off in a huff after grabbing the paper out of my hands.

"Some people have no sense of humor," I grumbled as I slung my beach basket over my shoulder so I could rub my freezing hands together.

It was time to cross the street and peddle papers on the other side. I was into the home stretch. My footsteps crunching the cold snow was the only sound I heard. Morning paper delivery is a lonely business.

Finally, I reached for the last paper, shoved it into the newspaper tube and was on my way home. My original plans of having a leisurely cup of tea with a good book and getting a two-hour head start on some long-overdue housework seeped out of my mind. Instead, slipping back under the covers for another hour of well-earned sleep seemed a much more appealing reward.

A few days after our newspaper adventure ended, my daughter's friend told her that his family was moving to California and he wanted her to take over the route.

Memories of 5:00 AM flashed before my eyes. "Count me out!" I said. "I donated my services for one week only. I can think of lots of things I'd rather do than get up at five AM every day. Jump off a cliff, acupuncture, childbirth . . ."

"Okay, Mom, I'll do it alone," my daughter said.

"I'm sorry, dear," I replied. "Get your brother or sister to help you. I need the sleep. Besides, mother love goes only so far. Not one bit further than five days on a paper route at five in the morning!"

Life's Too Short
to Worry about
Having Kids after Fifty

ONE THING'S FOR SURE. When you marry a man seventeen years older than you are and he's about an inch away from his fiftieth birthday, the subject of *more* children doesn't crop into normal conversation. His six and my three from our previous marriages were quite enough, thank you. But surprise, surprise!

When the pregnancy test came back positive, I was a little hesitant to tell Harold. Hesitant? I was terrified. How do you tell a man who's dreaming of early retirement that he's about to bring into the world a member of the college graduating class of 2003 and the 1980s haven't even started yet?

Almost apologetically I broke the news. The way Harold responded, you'd have thought he was a thirty-year-old who'd been trying to father his first child for years. That very afternoon he rushed out to buy cigars and started handing them out to his friends.

Perhaps he thought about how babies bring on a feeling of perpetual youth. Or maybe he thought that having one of our own would really solidify our marriage. He'd probably seen that old Lucille Ball movie *Yours, Mine and*

Ours. Perhaps he was just glad he still had what it takes to become a father. Whatever it was, dear Harold stomped through the tulips with glee when I told him the news.

For the first two and a half years after we were married, Harold's job kept him in Wisconsin during the week while my three children and I continued to live in northern Illinois. Of course, we were together every weekend, but when I became pregnant my heart broke when I learned the childbirth classes at our local hospital were only on Tuesday nights.

Harold had never been present during the birth of his other six children, and I wanted him to experience the incredible joy and miracle of childbirth. But unless he took childbirth classes, the hospital staff wouldn't consider him fit for delivery room duty.

Undaunted by the miles between us, Harold signed up to take childbirth classes by himself at a large hospital in Milwaukee. There he was, fifty-one years old, graying around the temples, sitting alone on the floor, week after week, learning how to pant and blow, pant and blow. He had to do some pretty fast talking to convince his classmates that he even *had* a pregnant wife.

When Andrew was born, Harold was a trouper. He coached and encouraged me through labor. In the delivery room, he all but delivered the baby himself . . . even talked the doctor into letting him cut the umbilical cord.

For a man who had paced the hospital halls with a headache during the birth of his other children, I was extremely proud of his delivery room technique. He held our son, posed for pictures and developed a bond with Andrew within minutes of his birth.

As Andrew grew, I noticed that although Harold did not get down on the floor and roughhouse with his young son as much as a younger man might, he and Andrew maintained that closeness initiated at birth.

Harold survived the terrible twos and the temper-tantrum-threes better than I did. Perhaps it was innate grandfatherly wisdom, learned from watching his half-dozen grandkids, that reminded him that all stages, no matter how exasperating, eventually pass.

Harold also remembered what it had been like when his first brood was at home. Trying to support six children under eleven years of age on a 1950s teaching salary of about five thousand dollars a year gave him ulcers. But as a newly promoted high-school principal he didn't have to worry whether his paycheck would cover the grocery bills.

When Andrew started school, his dad entered a new phase of life, including senior citizen discounts. But in spite of his advancing years, Harold had no trouble keeping up with the younger generation. In the summer he and Andrew visited the zoo, took walks along the lake, and played catch. In the winter Harold instructed Andrew on the fine points of giving Dad good back and foot rubs in front of the TV. Andrew's reward was usually a big bowl of popcorn and a piggyback ride to bed.

Naturally, there were days when Andrew put a vise-like strain on Harold's good nature. Like when Andrew hauled out his toy guitar and drums and made like Buddy Holly during the ball game on TV or during one of Harold's favorite old-time movies. Or when Andrew's unbridled energy and unreserved playtime sound effects broke the sound barrier. But then those were the times Andrew drove me up a skinny-limbed tree, too . . . so Harold's age was not a factor there.

Sometimes, though, Harold would think wistfully about retirement. Many of his contemporaries were planning to retire in four or five years. They talked about traveling and taking life easy. The words *condominium*, *Sun City* and *motor home* punctuated their conversations. But not Harold. As he approached sixty, he was still traveling to Little League games, music lessons, parent-teacher meetings and the orthodontist.

Often when Harold ran into an old friend the conversation usually went something like this:

"This little guy your grandson, Harry?"

"No, this is Andrew, my son."

"Oh yeah? *Heh, heh, heh.*"

Harold just laughed it off. Sometimes he laughed so hard he cried. Sometimes he just said, "Why me, Lord?"

Everything considered, I'd have to say that a man in his fifties can definitely father a child with little worry about whether or not he can handle it. Harold always remembered the old saw, "Age is simply a matter of mind. If you don't mind, it doesn't matter."

When Andrew was nine years old, his sixty-one-year-old father died of leukemia, a disease that can strike at any age. But in spite of losing his father at a young age, Andrew has good memories of his older dad . . . the Grandpa who became a Daddy and loved every minute of it.

Life's Too Short
to Sweat the Small Stuff

IT'S 5:30 PM, a dark winter weeknight. The odor of one of my *which-one-is-it-this-time* casseroles wafts through the kitchen and into the living room, drawing the entire family into a flurry of pre-meal activity, all within twenty feet of me.

I'm cutting vegetables for a salad. Harold, my just-home-from-work spouse, is seated at the breakfast counter engrossed in the evening paper, oblivious to the noise around him.

Jeanne is practicing the piano just a few feet away. She's now on page two of "Für Elise" for the ninth time.

Julia is doing what she does best . . . three things at once: (1) setting the table at breakneck speed, (2) listening to her favorite station on a small portable radio strapped to her waist (*It helps drown out the noise from the piano, Mom!*), (3) intermittently telling her dad about the sleep-over party her best friend is having and asking if she can interview him for her unit in careers. He grunts a noncommittal response to every other question and proceeds to the sports page.

Michael answers the third phone call in ten minutes, relays the message, then goes on with his riddle onslaught.

(*Will the person who gave eleven-year-old boys the right to read riddle books please stand up?*)

Andrew knocks over his tower of blocks stacked chimney high in the middle of the kitchen. (*It's the only place that isn't carpeted, Mom.*) Then he starts beating through my end-of-the-day headache on his new drum, with harmonica in mouth. The harmonica falls to the floor as he hollers in his loudest three-year-old voice, "I'm hungry! I want a drink! Can I have an apple?"

I flip on the garbage disposal, which at that moment seems a sensible addition to the cacophony at hand. Somewhere in my head I hear a little voice saying, "Why me, Lord?" The voice gets louder. "Lord, I can't stand this noise! I'm tired! I want to escape!" I wonder where that white knight is . . . the one who charges into your kitchen and whisks you off to dinner in a plush, quiet and oh-so-relaxing restaurant.

I reach for another green pepper in the refrigerator. As the door swings shut, my eyes catch one of the many pictures magnetized to the shiny white front. The hand-drawn big blue boy with a toothy grin is more scribbled than drawn. A giant, tilted *A* for Andrew next to the boy proclaims the artist's signature.

"Mommy! I'm hungry!" the artist screeches.

"Andrew, I'm fixing supper as fast as I can. Here, eat this carrot."

"No! I want supper! All the food!"

"Andrew, don't yell like that. I'm tired and hungry, too!" I explode. "You can wait like the rest of us."

At that moment Julia bounces into the kitchen and in her brightest diplomatic cheerleader voice says, "Hey, Mom, where'd you get that picture? The one on the wall. It's new, right?"

"*Huh?* Oh, that. I bought it today at the rummage sale at church."

"It's neat. The colors match the kitchen."

My shoulders sag a little when I remember what's written on the plaque. "Read it. I wonder if we match the words," I say somewhat sadly.

Julia clears her throat and in her most theatrical twelve-year-old voice booms, "We need one another, love one another, forgive one another. We play together, work together, grow together. God made us a family."

"Did God have to make us such a noisy family?" I growl.

Just then I feel a warm arm sliding across my shoulders. Harold reaches for the salad, puts it on the table and calls the troops to dinner.

We bow our heads. "Dear Lord," he says, "we certainly do need one another, love one another, forgive one another. We thank You for letting us work together, play together and grow together. We thank You for this family and for this food. Amen."

Silently I add my own prayer. *Lord, help me to keep my temper in tow. Help me step outside the circle of pandemonium this family creates and see my kitchen for what it really is. A place for all of us to huddle back together after a busy day apart. A place to spill out parts of our day to an audience of loved ones. A place to do those things that must be done at 5:30.*

I take a deep breath, smile at my husband and each of my four children, then reach for the green beans. I think to myself, *Yes, indeed, we are a family . . . especially at 5:30 on a winter weeknight.*

Life's Too Short to Get Old

WHEN MY FORMER FATHER-IN-LAW died in 1996, I was surprised to remember that I hadn't seen the man for more than twenty years. But during their growing-up years, my three older children, who were his grandchildren, made the trip to West Virginia with their father every couple of years to see their grandparents.

I remember my father-in-law in the 1970s, sitting at the kitchen table, with no shirt on, hungover and smoking one cigarette after another while he ordered his wife and children around, brutalizing them with his caustic and abusive remarks. I was afraid of him in those days. As a young bride, newly married to his oldest child, I didn't feel comfortable in his house, let alone around his hungover nastiness. I'd been raised in a strong, loving family and had never even been around an alcoholic in my life. *Naive* was my middle name, and that man scared the dickens out of me.

I heard over the years, however, that my ex-father-in-law mellowed somewhat. His wife never left his side, and he eventually stopped drinking. I wouldn't say theirs was a happy marriage, but I think as my ex-father-in-law grew older he at least became tolerable. I always hoped that he would finally figure out that his devoted wife was a saint for putting up with his abuse during those earlier years. Perhaps in his old age he tried to make it up to her.

At any rate, when he died, I started thinking about some other older people I know. I wondered if they, like my ex-father-in-law, thought of life as a burden. Are the ones whose lives seem to have no joy or meaning ready to be turned over to Dr. Kevorkian? I think not.

Great-Aunt Peggy was born in 1900. She lived in a nursing home in northern Illinois in the same community with her only living relatives: her nephew (my eighty-two-year-old dad), her niece (my ninety-three-year-old Aunt Helen), and dozens of great nieces and nephews until her death at age one hundred in 2001. Peggy was nearly blind, hard of hearing, very frail and often as cantankerous as they come.

A few years ago Dad and Aunt Helen went shopping to buy Peggy a new bathrobe. Because she was extremely picky about everything, they asked her exactly what type of bathrobe she wanted. They shopped and shopped until they found the perfect one and then had to pay lots more than they expected for it. When they gave it to her, she said it was fine. But the next few times they went to visit her in the nursing home, it was nowhere to be seen.

Dad finally asked, "Why don't you wear your new robe, Peggy?"

"Oh, it's too long. And the sleeves get in my way. And you know I can't stand collars," she groused.

Dad felt his blood pressure rise, then said, "Well, if you don't like it, why don't we just take it back to the store?"

"Can't do that," Peggy chided. "Already wrote my name in the collar . . . for the laundry people, you know."

"Well, then let's give it to Bernadine [Dad and Helen's sister]. She said the other day she needed a new robe," Dad suggested, desperately trying to salvage the situation.

Peggy harrumphed and said, "No, you just leave it here."

Next time Dad and Helen went to visit, he asked to see the expensive blue bathrobe so he could decide what should be done. When he opened the closet door, much to his blood-pressure-spiking consternation, he saw that Peggy had taken scissors and cut a foot off the bottom of the robe. Then she'd cut the sleeves up to the elbows. And the final insult was the fact that she had cut the beautiful, lace-trimmed collar completely off.

Dad was furious. "Where are your scissors! I'm taking them home! You have no business cutting up your clothes like this!" With that, Dad grabbed Peggy's scissors from the chest by her bed and stomped out the door.

The next time he and Helen visited, they were amazed to see Peggy wearing the ratty-looking bathrobe. But it wasn't so ratty looking. One of the nursing aids on Peggy's floor had taken the robe home, evened up Peggy's cutting job, and stitched new hems on the bottom, sleeves and collar. Peggy was as happy as a flea in a warm dog's back, enjoying her new robe with style and gusto.

Dad and Helen have gotten a lot of mileage out of that story, and by now they think it's pretty funny. Which just goes to show you . . . our oldsters may be crotchety and hard to please, but we must never forget that getting old is not easy. The aches and pains alone would make anyone hard to get along with. We *all* get crabby when we don't feel well. And when the only thing new and different in your life is a new-fangled bathrobe and that's all you have to think about day after day, who wouldn't want to be a little creative by customizing it just the way you want?

Another one of my favorite older people is Gert Adams. I met her when she was in her mid-seventies, and as spry and feisty as they come. In 1996 I had the privilege of being a co-chaperone with her as we escorted twenty-six teenagers through Germany for two weeks with the help of two teachers from our local high school. Gert's granddaughter Cheryl was one of the teenagers, and since Gert has relatives in Germany, she not only provided the financial means for Cheryl to go, she volunteered to go along as one of the chaperones so she could also visit her relatives. As we planed, trained and bused our way through "the old country" and shared hotel rooms, Gert and I got to know each other quite well.

One of the best conversations we had was when Gert told me about the time she had to move in with her daughter, son-in-law, two granddaughters and grandson for the second time while recuperating from ankle surgery. Gert's oldest granddaughter Holly, who was seventeen years old at the time, wrote a poem about the adventure of having her grandma move back in again. Holly captured not only the exasperation of getting older, but the absolute joy and grand experience older people can bring to our lives. Here it is, as only a teenage granddaughter could write about her beloved grandma.

GRANDMA'S BACK

by Holly Williams

"Lightning doesn't strike twice" just isn't true at all.
Grandma is back to stay again, because of that same fall.
The rules were just the same, we told her simply to holler.
With coupon in hand she asked for prunes,
they were two for just five dollars!
She was shacked up on the couch again
and had control of the TV,
This meant no cartoons or soap operas,
and especially no MTV!
She'd rather watch the news all day,
on every single station,
But I knew what the prunes were for,
the pills that gave her constipation.
She also watched the History channel,
which was pretty hard to bear.
I don't see why she had to watch it,
I mean, heck, she was there!
We teased her all the time, and she didn't make a fuss—
But when we drank from her denture cup,
the joke was back on us.
They say her screws were falling out,
no, not out of her head,
Out of her leg, of course, so the doctor put in lead.
But she teaches us good morals,
and what is right and wrong,
Especially because we can't sneak in,
'cause she's up all night long.
I'm sure it's worse for Grandma, though,
I know I shouldn't get fed up.
I'd certainly rather take care of her, than be the one laid up!

Gert's granddaughter obviously inherited her grandmother's sense of humor. When it comes right down to the condition of getting old, if we think about all the people we know over seventy, the ones we like best are the ones with a great sense of humor. Life is all about learning to make light of our foibles and laughing at ourselves. When we learn to do that, growing old doesn't seem so scary.

Life's Too Short to Be the Boss

WHEN THE DOORBELL RANG at Bud Morgan's son's house that Christmas Eve in 1991, he heard his son Jerry shout, "Tom! Come in! Wow, this is the greatest Christmas present ever! Dad! Look who's here!"

Bud was so shocked he could hardly move. There in the doorway was his younger son. He had neither seen nor spoken to Tom in over a year and a half, ever since the fight they'd had in Bud's office.

As the president and general manager of Wixon Fontarome, a spice and specialty foods company in Milwaukee, Bud was eager to groom both of his sons into management positions at Wixon. Jerry was working out fine. He enjoyed the work, learned quickly and was well on his way to a top slot, following in his dad's footsteps. Tom was a different matter. A free spirit who'd majored in journalism in college, he never did seem to enjoy the work. All he talked about was sports. Any books he ever read were about that topic.

One day Bud called him into his office. "Tom, you have to shape up. You're not focused or driven like you should be. You have to put your heart into this business. Thanks to my management savvy, I've turned this place around and now it's your turn to put your all into it! We've got a great company, but you're not holding your own. I hand you a terrific career, and you act like you don't care if we meet projections or not! You . . ."

Tom interrupted, "Dad, you know what? This is your business, not mine. It's *your* dream, *your* work. Everything has to be *your* way or *no* way. You think you're the only one who can do everything right. You intimidate people! And if you want to know the real truth, you're a pain in the neck to your employees *and* to your family!"

Tom turned around, walked out of the room and out of his father's life. Bud felt as if he'd been slapped in the face by his twenty-eight-year-old son. He was sure Tom didn't have the slightest idea of what he would do with his life when he walked out that door.

A few months later Bud and his wife Joanie heard from a friend that Tom had registered at the University of Wisconsin graduate school to get his master's degree in journalism. They tried to locate him but had no luck. Bud lost himself in his work—ten, twelve, often sixteen hours a day—and tried to forget about the problem with Tom. Joanie, who was used to Bud's workaholic schedule, begged him to slow down. But as the company and family control master, Bud didn't let her pleadings phase him. He worked harder and harder. Longer hours. More sales. Bigger projections.

Then, out of the blue, on that Christmas Eve, Tom walked back into their lives. Bud's prodigal son had come home. After hugs and tears and lots of "catching up,"

Joanie, Tom and Bud decided to take a trip together. They needed to mend fences, plan the future and bond back into a family.

Bud rented a house in Florida for two weeks, and the three of them took off on January 23. By three o'clock that afternoon they were just south of Louisville, Kentucky, when Bud stopped at a rest area, left the motor running in the van and jumped out to make his first of what would certainly be many phone calls back to the company. *After all,* Bud thought, *who else but me can maintain control of the place?* Bud spoke to Sandy, his vice president of administration.

"How are the orders going, Sandy? Did Jerry redo that report? Is everybody else doing their job? How about the new guy, is he getting organized?"

After thirty minutes of issuing directives and catching up on the seven hours he'd been away from the office, Bud got back behind the wheel of the van and they continued south. Twenty minutes later Joanie was asleep on the bench seat in the back, Tom was sound asleep in the front passenger seat, and Bud . . . well, he fell asleep behind the wheel. The van veered off the road, rolled over twice and crashed into a stone embankment. All three of them were thrown from the van and lay bleeding and broken.

After being rushed to the hospital in Louisville, they learned that Joanie had a broken pelvis and serious bladder damage. Tom had a burst colon, broken pelvis and shattered fourth through sixth vertebrae, rendering him paralyzed from the waist down. He was given a ten percent chance of living. Bud had a fractured left leg, broken neck and pelvis.

As the nightmare unfolded on three floors of the Humana Hospital in Louisville, Bud prayed, "Lord, help me to heal quickly, so I can help take care of Joanie and Tom when they get out of here." He begged and pleaded with God to fix things, so he could get their lives back in control.

He tried to be positive. He was, after all, the leader of a great company. He could forge ahead and conquer this. He'd listened to hundreds of motivational tapes and read inspirational books all his life. *Surely*, he thought, *I can think of something that will turn this nightmare into something positive.* But all he felt was grief and guilt for having caused the accident.

The next morning two cheerful young interns came into Bud's room. "Hi, we're here to attach your halo. This device will keep your head from causing pressure on your spine."

"How do you attach it?" Bud asked.

"We just drill two holes into your forehead and two into the back. We bolt it right into your head."

After the drilling, which wasn't as bad as it sounds, they set the device on Bud's head and started tightening the bolts. "Just let us know when the pain gets so intense you can't stand it. That's how we know when to stop."

"What? No anesthetic?"

"If we dope you up, you won't be able to tell us when to stop."

Bud endured the procedure and later tried to relax in the bed in an upright position, when a nurse's aide came in with a breakfast tray.

"Good morning, Mr. Morgan! Isn't it a beautiful day?"

He wanted to strangle her.

"You get to have a real breakfast this morning. Let's see, we have a wonderful glass of orange juice and a nice piece of whole wheat toast. And what's this? Why look here, Mr. Morgan, it's a beautiful poached egg!"

Bud wanted to tell Ms. Happy to shove that whole breakfast in the trash can, but instead he said, "Look, lady, I don't eat eggs. I have to watch my cholesterol. I haven't had an egg in two years."

As soon as those words were out of his mouth, he started laughing. He laughed so hard he didn't even notice the pain from his halo. That sweet, happy aid wondered what was so funny. "Miss, my wife is in serious condition on the floor above me. My son is paralyzed from the waist down on the floor below me. I just had a halo drilled into my head because of serious spinal injuries. My company is probably going down the tubes, and I'm worried about my cholesterol? Let me have that egg!"

Bud Morgan devoured that poached beauty with more gusto than any meal he'd ever had in his life, because he knew that his worrying days were over. It took a poached egg for the good Lord to get him to understand that *he* wasn't in control of anything in his life.

A few days later Bud and Joanie were airlifted back home to Milwaukee to a larger hospital where they both had surgery. Six days after that, with a metal hoop around his waist to protect his spine, a cast on his leg and the steel halo still on his head, Bud left the hospital to recuperate at home in a wheelchair.

All this time, ever since the day of the accident, Wixon Fontarome was running more smoothly than he could possibly have dreamed. His managers Chuck, Jerry, Larry and Sandy had met regularly and somewhat reorganized the company into a team system. They all knew they'd have to work together to make it run well. Every employee—from food scientists to chemists, office staff to production workers—joined that team. They kept orders on track and quality high. Customer expectations were met and, in fact, production went up. Their European partners and markets were reassured that the company was doing fine without Bud. None of the employees missed a beat during those months as they worked and barnstormed heaven with prayers for Bud, Joanie and Tom's recovery.

When Bud was finally able to go back to work, instead of being at the office seventy hours a week, he put in twenty hours and spent the rest of his time in a labor of intense love, caring for Joanie and Tom, who by that time were also home from the hospital. Bud and Joanie had a house built for their son right next to theirs, attached at the garage. Every morning and evening Bud relieved the workers who came in to help Tom. As a paraplegic, Tom needed help with the most basic bodily functions.

Tom and Bud shared those hours each day, and Bud began to notice a dramatic change in their relationship.

Bud had once heard on a motivational tape, "When the student is ready, the teacher will appear." Bud was ready to learn and Tom was his teacher.

"Dad, you know my friend Gary, the one I met in the hospital, the paraplegic? Why don't we take him to a baseball game? We'll take Mom, too. We can fit three wheelchairs in the van."

And so off they went to see the Brewers, laughing their way through one comical event after another as Bud figured out ways to negotiate three wheelchairs up to the mezzanine level of Milwaukee's County Stadium.

As he watched Tom master the most basic skills all over again, Tom taught his dad about patience. They talked about life and love and sports. Tom became his dad's best friend, his mentor.

Bud learned that neither a company nor a family is made up of one great leader who is in control of everything and everybody. Tom taught his dad to enjoy people and that time spent with those you love is what is really important. Joanie and Bud went for walks together and talked more. He told her every day how much he loved her and how much he admired her spirit. Through his love of sports, Tom taught his dad about teamwork. Bud learned that a company is a *group* of people who work together to make good things happen. A few months later, Bud took all 150 members of the Wixon Fontarome team and their spouses to Disney World for a four-day vacation, so they could laugh, play and really get to know one another.

In 1994, just two years after the accident, Tom died of

blood poisoning. During those two years he had never once complained about anything, not his pain, his discomfort or his disability. Instead, he had thrown himself into helping others through the rough times. He had started a mail-order business, began lifting weights, and made more friends and touched more lives than most people do in a lifetime.

Tom never once blamed his dad for the accident. Instead, at the time in Bud's life when he was forced to give up control of everything he held dear, Tom taught Bud how to slow down, spend more time with his family, friends and coworkers, and *let the team do the work*. It was a plan Bud Morgan, who died in 2001 of cancer, used for the rest of his life.

Chapter Two

Friendly Encounters

Without a doubt it's those special moments when someone or something pops into your life that is so outstanding, so amazing, so inspirational that you just have to stand there, shake your head and say, "Golly." Only you have to stretch out that "golly" with a long Southern drawl as Gomer Pyle did. Gaaaaa-uullll-yyyyy. These magical friendly encounters are just about the best thing on earth—right up there with warm chocolate chip cookies—to make you feel that you're in the presence of God. Amazing encounters with spectacular people keep our lives from becoming blah, save us from mediocrity, and prove once and for all the existence of angels. Life's too short not to welcome such wonders with gusto and grace.

Life's Too Short to Complain about Gifts

DON'T MOST WIVES GET FLOWERS or candy and maybe, every twenty-five years or so, real diamonds? Don't most husbands surprise their mates with gold earrings or nice clothes or, more often, a night out on the town on special occasions? Of course they do.

Why then did my hubby have to be so darn practical? He called it *creative*, but I think it bordered on spousal gift abuse. His idea of a great birthday gift for me was matching Tupperware bowls or a year's supply of cotton balls. Once I got a ball-point pen that was also a flash-light, a fingernail file and a corkscrew. The pen was handy, but once when I was filing my nails the flashlight accidentally turned on and I nearly corkscrewed a hole right into the sofa.

One Christmas, this man, with whom I had shared my life and four children for nine years, came up with match-ing maroon and yellow jackets for the two of us. The main problem, other than the fact that they were uglier than a mud fence, was that they were both men's sizes. His was a man's extra-large, mine a man's large. Granted, I did inherit my Grandmother Knapp's large bone structure, but in that jacket I looked like a Green Bay Packer across the shoulders

37

and the sleeves crept down to my knuckles. I returned mine to the catalog center and the next year he gave his to his brother.

The following Valentine's Day hubby came downstairs with his "I have a surprise for you" grin. He could never keep a secret for longer than ten minutes, and before I finished flipping the pancakes he whisked me upstairs to see my Valentine gift.

My eyeballs nearly popped out of my head. In one- to two-foot intervals, all along the walnut paneling in our bedroom, hubby had screwed in six pink plastic finger hooks. They were bad replicas of curved index fingers protruding obscenely from the wall. I looked at his face to see if perhaps it was a joke. "See, honey, you can hang your bathrobe on this one over here, your pajamas on that one, your bath towel here and your clothes over there if you don't feel like hanging them in the closet." His face was radiant.

All I could do was nod my head. Those hooks were so awful I decided to take them to the next "tackiest gift" party we attended. After a couple of weeks of seeing my clothes hanging all along the bedroom wall I think even hubby, the gadget guru, was glad to see those pink pointers removed.

That man loved to order things from mail-order catalogs. In fact, I'd say he was definitely addicted to them. There were always ten or fifteen catalogs stacked next to his easy chair in the family room, ready for the master to grab his pen and the mail-order forms. During our marriage

I received more gifts from Sunset House, Walter Drake, StarCrest and Carol Wright than I care to recall. He was also hooked on special offers in the Sunday newspaper and the backs of cereal boxes. We ate more cereal than should have been humanly possible to consume because he could order some cheap plastic gizmo for one of the kids.

One ad on his favorite brand of dry cereal said, "Guaranteed fresh flowers delivered to your home for Mother's Day." He could hardly wait to fill out that coupon and make a big impression. I knew that because I overheard him mumbling, "Oh, great idea for Mother's Day" in that sort of trance he got into when he picked up his catalogs each night.

The long corrugated cardboard box arrived with my name on it on the Monday *before* Mother's Day. The outside label said the box had been shipped by truck from California. We lived in Illinois at the time. It also said that the truck had left its departure point two weeks earlier. The flowers inside the box were the sorry remains of what resembled long stemmed pink carnations. They were just lying there in that box with no water, no preserving agents and no tissue paper to prevent them from beating up against the cardboard sides. Those Mother's Day carnations were dried up, matted and even had a sickening decaying odor surrounding them.

Luckily "Mr. I'll Order Anything" was out of town for the week and never knew the condition of those flowers. I just kept telling myself over and over, "It's the thought that counts."

After that brief stint with flowers, hubby went back to being practical. The next year for Christmas there was a twelve-foot-long Stanley tape measure in my Christmas stocking. I have to admit that it was nice not to have to go rummaging through his toolbox in the garage every time I wanted to measure something. But it was just the idea of getting a tape measure for a Christmas gift that was a bit unsettling.

Then there was the cute green plastic door mat he surprised me with on my birthday shortly after we bought our first house. It had a nice romantic touch. In bright red letters the mat said, TRUE LOVE IS JERRY AND PAT. It would have been an okay gift except that hubby's name was Harold, not Jerry. But he said they had it on sale at the hardware store and at least he got my name right. After one too many people asked me who Jerry was, I finally put the thing at the back door where only the neighborhood kids could see it.

One time I gave the gift meister a big hint right before Christmas. I said I sure could use some writing pens. He must have thought I said, "riding pants" because that's what I got. Brown wool pants with leather inserts in the inner thighs. He didn't even bother to ask me if I was planning to take up horseback riding before he let his fingers do the shopping. I should have known something was amiss when I saw him leafing through a new catalog with horses on the cover and all sorts of saddles, leather goods, bridles, even hay bales inside. In spite of the fact that we did go horseback riding on our honeymoon, I haven't been on a horse since.

The next year on our anniversary he hauled a huge box out of the car trunk. It was bigger than a microwave, more powerful than a locomotive, able to leap tall buildings. You guessed it. A snowblower. All heart, that guy.

What was it I said before about flowers, candy and diamonds for gifts? I've had it with flowers, at least the kind you order off the back of cereal boxes. Candy, well, that's fattening and bad for my teeth. Diamonds? All they do is sit there and sparkle. Besides, I know I'd worry like crazy if I left the house with anything on my body more valuable than the cost of the insurance deductible.

Even though that hubby has long since gone to his eternal reward, I still think about those hours and hours that he sat in his easy chair, pencil in mouth, pondering—page after page, catalog after catalog—what it was he wanted me to have. Some years at Christmas I'd have a dozen boxes to unwrap. Granted, most of those boxes contained things like gelatin molds, bread racks, wicker baskets, cookie sheets and other obnoxious kitchen gadgets, but at least he never forgot my birthday, or any occasion for that matter. Why, he even bought me gifts on St. Patrick's Day. I miss that man . . . the gift meister extraordinaire.

Life's Too Short to Be Too Attached to Animals

"I'M NOT TOO CRAZY ABOUT ANIMALS," I told my new neighbor, the day after we moved to Wisconsin. I looked down at her big dog, Woofer, who was licking my foot.

The words tumbled out of my mouth so matter-of-factly that I winced. For the past twenty years I'd turned the disappointments and broken hearts I'd experienced with animals into a dislike for creatures in general.

I remembered back to third grade, the year my very first pet, the big gray fluff-ball cat, came to live with us. Susie loved to jump over the garden hose while I raised up one end like a crooked hurdle. She and I played outside in the thick summer grass, chasing balls and dandelion puffs. Then, just a few months later, Susie became ill. The vet told Dad the kindest thing would be to put her out of her misery. At my cousin's farm that evening, I pretended to be interested in the new colt and the barn full of baby pigs, but I heard the single shot and knew Susie was no longer my best friend.

Next came the turtles. Dad bought an old tractor tire from a farmer, painted it red and set it in concrete in the backyard. Then he built forms for a foot-wide circular sidewalk around the giant tire. When the cement mixture was still wet, he carved the words, "Pat's Turtle Ranch" on the front. Inside the tire, Dad molded hills and valleys in the wet cement and even provided sun-bathing places for the turtles with cypress logs.

Pete and Repeat, a couple of shy, two-inch-diameter turtles made their debut in "Pat's Turtle Ranch" as soon as the concrete hardened. They sunbathed, dove in and out of the water, and played with me daily for most of the summer. One morning, however, I couldn't find either turtle.

Later that afternoon Dad shook his head slowly, sadly. "Must have been a raccoon on the prowl last night. Sorry, honey. I'll see if I can find you a big old land turtle to plop in there."

Sure enough, a few days later, after scouring the gravel roads on his rural mail route, Dad spotted a hard-shelled beauty, ten times the size of Pete and Repeat. This one I named Marble Mabel because of the beautiful variegated pattern on her underside shell.

Marble Mabel disappeared after two weeks in the turtle ranch. "She must have climbed from the cypress log up to the tire and then rolled down to the grass," Dad explained.

That winter, two dime-store goldfish, Henny and Penny, flipped and flopped in a large bowl in our living room picture window.

Did I overfeed them? Were they sick to begin with? Those two gold-orange beauties, one with a black stripe across her gills, lasted just under two months.

"Mama, Penny's dead!" I screamed when I bent over to

feed my fish. Henny swam lethargically without purpose after Mother scooped Penny out and flushed her down the toilet. Mother called it "burial at sea."

The next day I had to mourn all over again when I found Henny belly-up. "Animals don't like me and I don't like them!" I whined in bed that night.

"Of course they like you, Pat," Mother tried to comfort. "Sometimes it's just their time to die and you must let them go. Other animals will fill up your heart."

"No more animals!" I insisted.

A few weeks later, Easter morning dawned warm and holy. There before my eyes were two real, live, tiny, peeping, fluffy, baby chickens. Those newborn chicks helped define something truly sacred and hopeful about the Easter season for my ten-year-old psyche that year.

Patience and Prudence (I hoped they were girl chickens) became my sole responsibility. I fed those chicks, exercised them, chased them, cuddled them, talked to them and watched them sprout from yellow-cuddly-cute to gray-gangly-awkward . . . but still beautiful in my eyes.

Toward the end of the summer, Patience and Prudence started squawking and flapping their wings at the slightest provocation. Dad said, "They just don't like that small cage, Pat."

A few weeks later when the squawking became unbearable, Dad said we had to take my beloved feathered friends out to McCue's farm where they'd be infinitely more content in the enormous white clapboard chicken coop with the other chickens. Six months later, after fattening up his brood, Frank McCue, a high-school classmate of my dad's and a seasoned grain and livestock farmer and father of nine, mentioned to Dad, "Had those two hens you brought out to the farm last fall for dinner Sunday. Mighty fine eating."

I didn't sleep well for a week after that, and decided once and for all that I was through with animals. I'd had enough heartbreaks, thank you.

For the next twenty years neither mammal, reptile, fish nor fowl found its way into my heart. And so here I was, a grown woman with four children telling my new neighbor that I didn't really like animals, but in the same breath I assured her that my kids were crazy about them. A few weeks later she asked me if we would keep Woofer for a few days while her family was on vacation.

"Keep Woofer?" I stammered aloud. To myself, I thought, *In our home? No way! Animals and I don't get along!*

The olds wounds resurfaced. Susie, Pete, Repeat, Marble Mabel, Henny, Penny, Patience and Prudence all flashed before my eyes.

Aloud to my new neighbor I heard foreign words coming out of my mouth. "Oh sure, we'd be glad to take Woofer."

My children were overjoyed. They'd been begging for a dog for a dozen years. Of course, I'd known better than to let them have an animal who would just break their hearts in the long run. I figured I'd suffered enough for two generations.

Woofer arrived with his sleeping basket, his favorite chewed-up pink blankie, food and water dishes, canned dog food, and a list a page long of things to do for his dog-eared majesty. Within fifteen minutes, he had relieved himself in three different places in my house. "Oh, Lord, I *told* You I don't like animals!" I grumbled while I cleaned up the mess.

By the next morning the carpet was dry and the county zoo odor had dissipated. Even though Woofer had ignored his basket and pink blanket for his night's sleep, and chose instead the good living-room sofa, I tried to make friends with him.

But at mealtimes I just wasn't used to having soulful eyes and a wet wagging tongue perched expectantly six inches from my plate. Embarrassed to be eating in front of even a four-legged someone, I gobbled my food, then scraped the leftovers onto Woofer's dish. He devoured every morsel before I could get back to my chair. When I saw how Woofer enjoyed my cooking, I started genuinely to like that dog.

"Lord, maybe Your creatures aren't so bad after all." I could feel those old third-grade feelings coming on again.

A few months after Woofer left, another neighbor asked my son Michael to dog-sit Charlie for a few days. The first day I lavished Charlie with two and a half bowls of my special seafood bisque, a rich cream soup loaded with salmon, tuna, shrimp and crab. I liked it, the kids hated it, but Charlie thought it was divine. Afterward I couldn't go anywhere without Charlie wagging his tail behind me.

Hey, I thought, *maybe I'm an animal lover after all!*

The next morning one of the kids announced that someone had up-chucked in the living room. The children said it looked like seafood bisque. *Figures*, I thought, putting on my old anti-animal shell.

Charlie looked a little sheepish, so I promised never to temp him into gluttony again. By the time Charlie left, the whole family, myself included, had grown attached to the big, friendly dog with the wagging tail.

At one point I even agreed to let Herbie the cat join our family on a permanent basis, or so we thought. A traffic accident a few months later tragically ended that relationship.

Our next animal venture, goldfish, repeated exactly the fish story of my youth, complete with burial at sea. And the two gerbils, who quickly became eight gerbils and then twelve gerbils, soon found their way to the high-school science department. I think they were going to be used to feed the department's huge boa constrictor, but I didn't tell the kids. What I told them was that God's creatures were gifts, however fleeting, and that we must give them up joyfully at the proper time. At that point I'd have said *anything* to get rid of those gerbils.

Next we tried rabbits, one at a time. The first was Barclay, the second, Minta Pearl, and the third, Lucy. Each one lived outside in a huge fenced pen the size of a room. At night they'd crawl into their little cage at one end of the pen. Season after season disaster struck. The neighbor's big German shepherd managed to get loose three times, tore into our yard, jumped the rabbit pen fence and did what dogs do naturally. He killed them with one quick snap of the neck.

I'm not sure if my heart ached more for our beloved rabbits or for Andrew, who had cherished each one with a gentleness I found amazing. By the time Lucy met her untimely death, I had to watch my son sitting in the middle of the pen, tears streaming down his face, totally at a loss as to why such things had to happen.

In the meantime, Michael continued to earn college money by periodically boarding dogs in our home for days and weeks at a time. And just as I had twenty-five years earlier, the children fell in love with each and every visitor.

Punkin was our all-time favorite. A happy, friendly, full-of-fun English springer spaniel, Punkin belonged to the principal of the grade school my children attended. For more than fifteen years, Mr. Winston trusted us with the care of his beloved dog every time he and his wife went on vacation.

Once, after having Punkin for more than a week, Andrew, who was five years old at the time, cried and cried when she left. Andrew had learned to whistle that week just so he could get the dog to follow him everywhere.

"Mommy, now when I whistle, nobody comes," Andrew sobbed after Punkin left.

I gathered my son to my lap and shared a Bible verse that sums up my whole philosophy about animals . . . a philosophy that has taken me nearly fifty years to get right.

> For everything there is a season, and a time for every
> matter under heaven:
> a time to be born, and a time to die;
> . . . a time to kill, and a time to heal;
> . . . a time to weep, and a time to laugh;
> a time to mourn, and a time to dance;
> . . . a time to seek, and a time to lose;
> a time to keep, and a time to cast away.
>
> ECCLESIASTES 3:1–4, 6 (RSV)

Life's Too Short
to Waste a Perfectly
Good Cold Day

WE AWOKE TO one of the coldest January days ever recorded in Milwaukee. The actual temperature was twenty-two degrees *below* zero, with a wind chill factor of seventy below. Most schools in southeastern Wisconsin were closed because the risk of frostbite was too great for children waiting for school buses.

We'd run out of wood for the wood burner during an earlier cold snap, and the furnace was running almost constantly. The house was still cold. I was wearing two pairs of pants, a turtleneck and a pullover sweater, and was still shivering in the kitchen as I wondered what Andrew, my youngest child (the only one still living at home) would do stuck in the house all day.

Just then my almost-six-foot-tall eighth-grader walked into the kitchen. As I rubbed my arms to ward off a chill, Andrew asked in a perfect English accent, "Say, Mum, don't you think it's 'bout time for a spot of tea?"

I laughed as I grabbed the tea kettle to fill it with water, remembering that Andrew was in drama class that semester and that he was fascinated with his Scottish,

Irish, English, French, German and Dutch ancestry, especially the different accents of each language. I looked closely at my son, whose father had died five years earlier, and was filled with awe at what a warm and easy relationship Andrew and I had developed over the years.

"Why certainly, my good man," I declared with as much drama as I could muster.

Andrew's eyes twinkled. He knew the scene was set. From that moment, neither of us spoke in our *real* voices. My English accent was muddled, but I tried hard to mimic the drama in Andrew's more perfected version. At any rate, we both became one hundred percent English subjects.

"Do you fancy a spot of Earl Grey or Jasmine? English Breakfast or Prince of Wales? What flavor grabs your fancy this brisk morning?"

"Say, Mum, I've always wondered. What is the difference between high tea and low tea?"

"Well, lad, low tea, which is usually called afternoon tea, is generally served at a low coffee or end table while the guests relax on a sofa or parlor chairs. High tea is served at a high dining room table in the early evening, our traditional supper hour. More substantial foods are served at high tea, you see."

As a woman who had never had a cup of coffee in her life but who was a fanatical tea drinker, I was enjoying this opportunity to draw my son into my wonderful world of tea drinking. I was also having fun trying to perfect my less-than-adequate English accent with every sentence.

Andrew rubbed his hands together as if warming

them over an old English kitchen fireplace. "So, Mum, perhaps we should have low tea on the coffee table in the living room. I'll make the preparations while you put the kettle on."

Before I had time to remind my son that I had work to do in my home office, Andrew cleared the magazines and newspapers off the low, round, oak coffee table closest to the sofa, grabbed a cotton lace runner in the dining room and spread it across the table. Then he retrieved a centerpiece of dried flowers from the marble-top chest in the hallway and placed it behind the lace runner.

Just weeks before, on Christmas morning, Andrew had proudly presented me with a small, solid oak mantle clock he'd made in technical education class. Of course, for today's occasion, my most treasured Christmas gift was removed from the fireplace mantle and placed between the centerpiece and the lace runner on the coffee table. The clock's rhythmic ticking, which could now be heard in the kitchen, made it seem that we were actually living in a drafty old English manor outside London.

Next, Andrew opened the doors of the china cupboard and retrieved my small English blue and white tea pot, two delicate, antique, hand-painted bone china teacups and saucers, two champagne glasses, the silver cream and sugar set, and a silver tray.

"I do declare, Mum, I can't see my face in the silver. It's in dire need of a good polishing."

"I'll get right on it, Master Andrew," I said with a wink as I turned off the stove with the pot of water on it. I could tell low tea was going to be a production of some magnitude that would require timely preparation, and there was no sense boiling the water now.

Andrew set the table with two sandwich plates trimmed with flowers and gold paint that he found behind the silver. Then, in the napkin drawer, he searched for two perfect ones, settling on dark green linen with a large hand-embroidered yellow maple leaf on each corner.

After retrieving the polish from under the sink, I demonstrated the fine art of silver polishing. The milk and sugar bowls sprang to exquisite shiny life as glittering silver emerged from black tarnish.

"Here, you finish polishing the silver tray while I make finger sandwiches, my good man."

"Finger sandwiches?" He looked at me as if I was one napkin ring short of a set.

"Yes, my English subject, finger sandwiches. Wee, dainty, open-faced sandwiches with the crusts cut off that you eat with your fingers. Tiny tidbits, three or four bites each."

"*Ah* yes. Charming, my good lady. Charming, indeed."

I wondered if Andrew's drama teacher had any idea of his ability to capture an accent with such insight and perfect use of phrasing and intonation.

I pulled cream cheese and cherry preserves from the refrigerator. I made triangles out of wheat bread and lathered on the preserves, making sure there were three or four actual cherries on each piece. Then I mixed the cream cheese with parsley, onion flakes, garlic powder and chives, and spread it on toasted rounds of French bread. I could see a definite look of approval on Andrew's face.

"Here, the tray is ready. Gleaming, don't you think?" he proclaimed proudly as a glint of his true English heritage shone through his eyes and his face was mirrored in the silver. I carefully arranged the sandwiches on the tray.

"What can we put in these tall fancy dishes, Mum?" my son quizzed as he dusted the cut glass champagne glasses that had hardly ever been used.

"A lovely fruit compote, don't you think? Here, slice this banana and I'll cut up an apple. We'll add kiwi, raspberries and fruit juice. It'll be fit for the Queen Mother herself," I beamed.

As we waited for the water to reheat, Andrew dashed off to his room where he scoured his childhood collection of 160 hats, hanging on all four walls, for a proper hat to wear to what was most certainly going to be a very proper low tea.

My handsome son emerged wearing an all-wool, green, yellow and white plaid tam with a snap-down front and a bright yellow pompon of clipped yarn on top. My godparents, Uncle Bob and Aunt Bernadine, had given it to Andrew after a trip they took to Scotland and England. Andrew had also slipped into an old floppy green herringbone sport coat I'd picked up at Goodwill to wear in my workroom on cold days. I stood back and looked at my son. The hat and jacket had transformed his tall, trim body into a gentleman as striking as an English lord.

"Mum, don't you suppose you need a proper hat and

skirt for the occasion?" he winked at me and shooed me off to my bedroom to change.

I glanced at my own five-piece hat collection and emerged with a simple beige wide-brimmed straw hat with a single feather protruding off to the side. To my cranberry-colored sweater I attached an antique round pin with multicolored stones that had belonged to Andrew's great-grandmother. A long black matronly skirt pulled on over my pants completed my outfit.

We were the perfect lord and lady. The tea kettle whistled. As I poured the boiling water into the proper tea pot and added loose black Darjeeling tea encased in a large chrome tea-ball, Andrew tuned the radio to a station playing classical music. He offered me his arm as we entered the living room.

As we made ourselves comfortable on the sofa, I wondered if getting ready for our tea party wasn't more fun than the actual event would be. I remembered, as a child, spending hours building a play house out of an enormous refrigerator-sized cardboard box. When completed . . . cut, colored and decorated . . . the fun was over.

But I needn't have worried. Andrew escorted me from the kitchen into the living room where everything was picture perfect, and we began an hour-and-a-half-long visit with each other that was as delightful as it was surprising.

By now, my character in our English play-acting had evolved into a sort of beloved great aunt who lived in a castle high on an English countryside and was absolutely delighted that her young nephew had dropped in for an unexpected visit. Suddenly, I wanted to know everything about this young man as I watched him carefully pour tea into the hardly-ever-used beautiful teacups.

"So, tell me, Sir Andrew, what are your plans? Where are you going in this great adventure of life?"

Andrew leaned back on the throw pillows as he sipped his tea and stroked his chin. "Well, it's a long road, you know. I still have four years of high school after this year, then college. Sometimes I wonder if I'll be able to afford college."

I reminded him that financial aid would be available just as it had been for his older sisters and brother. We talked about how he might get into one of his dream schools if he kept up his grades.

We slid into conversation about girls. Andrew looked out the floor-to-ceiling windows into the barren tree tops and said slowly, "The girls. I think they all think I'm a geek."

"Oh surely not! Why, Andrew, my good man, you're handsome, smart, funny. I bet the girls love you. You just don't know it yet."

Andrew continued to look out over the trees as he sipped the steaming tea. Then he turned and said, "I don't fight much, so they probably say I'm a wimp."

My eyes rested on Andrew's size thirteen feet, which proclaimed that his six-foot growth spurt was not over. I reassured him that not fighting was much more manly, something the high-school girls would certainly appreciate.

As time passed we talked about music, sports, weather, God and the school mixer coming up the next week. We watched a squirrel on the deck outside the windows eating corn off a cob. I told Andrew how scared I had been the year before, when I quit my regular job to stay home and work at my dream of being a writer. I told him I was lonely sometimes. "You know, it's hard being here alone all day in this big old house. I miss Jeanne, Julia and Michael. All grown. All in college. Can you believe it, Andrew?"

He nodded, poured a tiny bit of skim milk into his tea and picked up another sandwich. I took a deep breath and continued, "Someday I'd love to meet a wonderful, interesting man with a great sense of humor and deep faith." I looked into the eyes of my son, who was pretending to be my grown-up nephew in drafty old England and said, "I'd like to get married again someday, Andrew. I don't want to grow old alone."

The cold morning turned warm and wonderful as we each took turns talking and listening very intently to what the other had to say. We both revealed parts of ourselves that had always been hidden. Every so often Andrew poured more tea for each of us. As he picked up the tiny sugar tongs, he'd ask, "One lump or two, Mum?" Then he'd politely offer the plate of tiny sandwiches.

On that cold winter day, when I was forty-eight years old and Andrew fourteen, we were transported into a world we both knew would only exist for that one morning. When the next day came and school reopened, we would never again have a tea party like this one. Andrew would immerse himself in school, the basketball team, the junior high band, his friends, the school play, the telephone and video games at his best friend's house.

But it didn't matter because on that coldest day of the year, during those precious three hours as we stumbled through a mumble jumble of English phrases and inadequate but charming accents, my youngest child and I ate, drank, talked, shared, laughed and warmed our souls to the very core.

Andrew and I not only created a cherished memory, but we wrote and directed a play at the same instant we performed it. There was no audience. Just Andrew and me, and cups of very good tea.

Life's Too Short to Block Out the Voices Inside Your Head

I NEVER KNEW whether to pay any attention to those voices that pop into my head every once in a while, until I met Art, "The Swami of Origami" . . . so proclaimed on his business card. A friend had told me that Art was a professional chair caner, and I had an old rocking chair that needed a new cane seat. So when my friend gave me Art's business card, I was surprised to learn that he was also a creative paper folder.

When I arrived at his house with my rocker, I discovered a man of many talents. Not only was Art a children's librarian at a large branch of the Milwaukee Public Library, but he was a professional story teller and a children's hospital chaplain. His hobby, origami, was evident all over the house, as delicate and intricate birds, beasts, boxes, houses and ribbons of brightly colored folded paper were on display everywhere, forming borders along the ceilings in every room.

We talked about Art's paper folding and his job as chaplain at the hospital. We talked about life and people. I learned quickly that Art was a man of great feeling and zest for life. After making arrangements to pick up my chair in a week, he walked me to the door.

"Do you mind if I ask you a question?" he asked slowly.

"Not at all," I responded. Somehow I knew he was about to ask something important.

"Have you ever heard a little voice inside your head telling you to do something you didn't understand?"

"Well, I suppose so," I said slowly, not sure exactly what Art meant.

"Did you do what the voice told you?" he asked.

I was curious as to why he'd asked me this esoteric question, so I turned it around and asked him the same thing, "Have you ever heard a voice?"

"Yes, I have. And something amazing happened."

Art started at the beginning. A few months earlier, as a part-time origami teacher at the LaFarge Lifelong Learning Institute in Milwaukee, he was asked to represent the school at an exhibit at a large shopping mall in the area. He decided to take along a couple hundred paper cranes that he'd folded to give to people who would stop at his booth asking questions about origami.

A week before the event, however, Art heard a strange voice. It was inside his head, loud and clear, telling him over and over to find a piece of gold foil paper and to make a golden origami crane.

At first Art ignored the voice. He was, after all, a man with both feet on the ground, not given to hearing voices or believing in such strange phenomena. But the voice continued every day with the same simple request. *Find a piece of gold foil and make a golden origami crane.*

Art harrumphed and tried to ignore the voice. But then he found himself talking back to the voice. *Why gold foil anyway? Paper is much easier to work with.*

The voice continued to haunt him. Art continued to grumble. Finally, the night before the event at the mall, the voice was even more insistent and more specific. *Do it! Make a crane out of gold foil paper. And tomorrow you must give the golden crane to a special person.*

By now Art was getting cranky. *What special person? This is ridiculous! How will I know who the special person is?*

The voice continued, clear as a star-filled winter sky inside his head. *You'll know who the special person is,* the voice answered stoically.

Before his common sense voice could talk him out of it, Art went down to his basement shelves where he stored his collection of origami paper. He searched and searched until he found one piece of shiny gold foil paper six inches square.

That evening Art slowly, carefully, painstakingly folded and shaped the unforgiving gold foil until it became as graceful and delicate as a real crane about to take flight. He packed the exquisite bird in a large box along with about two hundred colorful paper cranes he'd made over the previous few weeks.

The next day at the mall, dozens upon dozens of people stopped by Art's booth. Youngsters, their parents, middle-aged people and senior citizens all asked questions about origami. Art demonstrated the art. He folded, unfolded, refolded. He explained the intricate details, the need for sharp creases. He created different animals and unusual shapes for his audience as they strolled by.

Then, toward the end of the day, there was an older woman standing in front of Art. He'd completely forgotten about the voice in his head that had bugged him during the previous week. But now, suddenly, he felt a warmth moving up from his toes to his eyebrows. He knew immediately that the woman standing in front of him was the special person.

Art had never seen her before, and she didn't say a word as she watched him carefully fold a bright pink piece of paper into a striking paper crane with pointed, graceful wings. Art glanced up at her face, and before he knew what he was doing his hands were in the big box that contained the supply of paper cranes. There it was, the delicate gold foil bird he'd labored over the night before. He retrieved it and carefully placed it in the woman's hand.

"I don't know why, but there's been a very loud voice inside my head for a week telling me that I'm supposed to give you this golden crane. The crane, by the way, is the ancient symbol of peace," Art said simply to the older woman.

The woman didn't say a word as she slowly cupped her small hand around the fragile bird as if it were alive. Art saw tears filling her eyes, ready to spill out.

Finally, the woman took a deep breath and formed her words slowly. "My husband died three weeks ago. This is the first time I've been out of the house since his funeral. Today ... today ..." The woman could hardly get the words out. She wiped her eyes with her free hand, still gently cradling the golden crane with the other.

In a moment, she continued. As she looked down at the golden bird, a hint of a smile came across her lips. She spoke very quietly, "Today . . . is our golden wedding anniversary."

Then the woman looked directly into Art's eyes as she placed her free hand on top of Art's own. In a clear voice she said, "Thank you for this beautiful gift. Now I know that my dear husband is at peace. Now I'm at peace. This bird, this symbol of peace, is God's messenger. Don't you see? That voice you heard ... it was the voice of God ... and this beautiful golden crane is a gift from the Almighty. It's the most wonderful fiftieth wedding anniversary present I could have received. Thank you for listening to the voice inside your head ... to the voice of God."

That's how my friend Art learned to listen very carefully when a little voice within him tells him to do something he may not understand at the time. And that's how Art convinced me to do the same. And I've learned that when you listen very carefully, it's amazing what you'll hear.

Life's Too Short
to Say, "I Can't Afford It!"

As WE WALKED UP the center aisle of the candlelit church, I could hear my three-year-old granddaughter Hailey *oohing* and *aahing* over the decorations. Huge Christmas trees with sparkling white lights nearly filled the sanctuary. A large rustic manger scene occupied the space in front of the altar. Giant sparkling gold stars dangled from the ceiling. Banners proclaimed the birth of Jesus as the choir sang softly, "Silent night, holy night."

I led my family—adult children, daughter-in-law, granddaughter and sixteen-year-old son—into the very first pew so that Hailey could see everything up close. We'd arrived a half-hour early for the Christmas Eve service at my insistence so that we could claim the first "bird's-eye view" pew.

As I snuggled into the end of the pew and pulled Hailey up onto my lap, I saw the angel for the first time. In front of the side altar, nestled in between three undecorated evergreens, was the most magnificent angel I had ever seen. *Where had it come from?* I wondered. Standing four feet tall with a three-foot wingspan behind her delicate body, the angel was wrapped in filmy bronze-green clothes. Hands reaching out in a welcoming gesture, her expression radiated peace and protection. This was, indeed, a magnificent angel. An angel of the Lord.

After the service began, our pastor moved to the pulpit near the angel and began to speak.

"I want to tell you about this angel," Father Ron said with a twinkle in his eye. "A few weeks ago my mother and I were browsing in a local mall. We wandered into a temporary store, set up just for the holiday season, which contained statues . . . original art pieces purchased from museums all over the world. Most of the stunning brass and bronze statues were life-size. Some over eight feet tall. All were breathtakingly beautiful.

"At the end of one aisle I glanced at the statue of an angel in front of me and then had to step back to get a better look. 'What a stunning piece of artwork,' I said to myself."

Father Ron looked out over the packed Christmas Eve congregation and continued, "I'd glanced at the prices of a few of those marvelous statues as we walked down the aisle. Thousands and thousands of dollars for each one! I wondered who could possibly afford to purchase such statues?"

As my little granddaughter squirmed off my lap and onto her mother's, my eyes drifted over to the angel again. *Is this the same angel Father is talking about?* I wondered. If so, she must have cost thousands of dollars. How could our small parish in South Milwaukee afford such an angel?

Father Ron's eyes glowed as he gestured toward the angelic creature, "When I saw this angel, I was mesmerized by her beauty and by her arms that reach out as if she's helping someone. I turned over the price tag. Seven thousand dollars! *Way beyond our means,* I thought.

"Just then a tall, striking gentleman of Middle Eastern descent, perhaps Arab, or maybe Indian or Pakistani, walked up to us. In broken English the man said, 'The angel, she is beautiful, yes?'

"I said, 'Yes, she is the most beautiful I have ever seen. We want to build a memorial shrine, but we don't have that much money to . . .' I stopped talking when I realized the salesman was no doubt of a different faith and perhaps wouldn't understand, much less care about, our needs at St. Mary's.

"The man spoke. 'Tell me again what it is you need the angel for.'

"'My parish. I am the pastor of St. Mary's Church in South Milwaukee. It's a small parish. Good, hard-working people, but we don't have much money. We want to build a memorial hospitality room in the back of church. A place where we can remember all the deceased members of our parish. A place to celebrate the living, too. We'll have a bulletin board for photos of weddings, baptisms, confirmations . . . and I, well, I've been hoping to find an angel to preside over this place of prayer and hospitality.'

"'I see,' said the tall, serious man with the wavy jet black hair. He pulled a calculator out of his pocket. 'My name is Ali,' he said slowly with particular emphasis on the second syllable. 'I am the owner and manager. We travel all over the country with these exquisite museum pieces.'

"Ali started punching numbers on his calculator. Then he cleared the total and started over. More numbers. He kept punching buttons and coming up with different totals."

Father Ron looked at the angel and took a deep breath before he continued. "I remember thinking, *Even if he gives us a discount of twenty, thirty or even fifty percent, we still can't afford this angel!* I'd already looked at angels in other stores, religious goods stores where three-foot-tall art reproduction angels made out of fiberglass cost more than two thousand dollars. I thought, *What am I doing here in a place where exquisite, original, one-of-a-kind pieces of artwork are on display?*

"I began to feel uncomfortable, wishing we'd passed by this store on our stroll through the mall.

"Finally Ali finished fiddling with the calculator. 'How does this look?' he asked as he held the calculator in front of my eyes. 'I will even deliver the angel to your church for you personally,' he said.

"My head jerked back a bit when I saw the figure. 'Sixteen hundred dollars? Are you sure? For this angel, the one priced at seven thousand dollars?' I had to be sure there was no mistake.

"'Yes. This one.' Ali touched the angel's wing. 'This cast bronze angel is signed by the artist. It is a masterpiece.'

"'But why?' It was all I could mutter as my imagination took flight. I knew we could afford sixteen hundred dollars. Some generous souls had already donated that much to our 'hospitality room fund.' Could it be possible that our little parish could own such an angel? I started to imagine the new room in greater detail. I could see the angel in the center of a room filled with comfortable furniture, where our parish family could feel the presence and love of all those who have been a part of our parish since it began in 1893.

"Ali continued. 'You ask why? It is because I, too, am a spiritual man. I am a Muslim. I would rather see this angel in a house of prayer than in someone's home. All I request is that on the day you put this angel in your church, you ask your people to pray for Ali.'"

Father Ron looked out over the congregation. "My friends, today Ali and his brother delivered this angel to St. Mary's and today I began to understand a little more about angels. I learned firsthand that not all angels are gilded with copper and bronze. Not all angels are named Michael or Gabriel. Today I learned that some of them are tall with dark hair and black mustaches. One of them is a Muslim named Ali."

At that moment the choir began to sing with grace and gusto, "Hark the herald angels sing, glory to the newborn king!" And everyone of us, from the front pew on back, bowed our heads and said a prayer for an angel named Ali.

Life's Too Short to Play It Safe

MY OLDEST DAUGHTER JEANNE hadn't been home for more than sixteen months. A lot had happened to her in that time. In the spring of 1996 she'd been accepted to Yale University for graduate school in fine art. Her boyfriend Canyon graduated from nursing school, and in the fall Jeanne and Canyon moved from California to New Haven, Connecticut, where Canyon got a job as an emergency room nurse and my daughter started classes at Yale.

Jeanne told me she wanted to come home for Christmas, but it was out of the question moneywise. Up to her eyelids in debt from her undergraduate studies, she was now facing even bigger college loans for her graduate work.

Shortly after Thanksgiving I called my daughter with great news. "Jeanne, I can get you and Canyon passes from one of the pilots who stay at our house. Of course you'll have to fly standby."

"No problem, Mom! We'll leave here on Saturday, December 21, and beat the Christmas rush. Thanks!"

A few weeks later, Jeanne and Canyon arrived at the ticket counter at Midwest Express Airlines at LaGuardia Airport in New York City at 5:30 AM after staying up all night packing and leaving New Haven at 3:00 AM By some miracle there were exactly two seats left on the plane after all the full-fare ticketed passengers were boarded. At 6:15 AM Jeanne and Canyon sauntered up the aisle of the DC-9 and slid into two side-by-side, extra-wide leather seats. Jeanne breathed a sigh of relief, knowing that in just two hours she'd be walking into my arms in Milwaukee.

"Jeanne Lorenz. Canyon Steinzig." Their names crackled on the intercom. As Jeanne fumbled for the flight attendant call button, a knot formed in her stomach. She raised her hand. "We're here," she said weakly.

The flight attendant walked up to their seats. "I'm sorry," she whispered. "You'll have to deplane. Two full-fare passengers just arrived at the gate. You'll have to give up your seats."

Jeanne knew the rules that went along with the passes. No complaining. No arguing. Wear nice clothes. Don't make waves. Do what you're told. Smile and act like those passes are the best thing since warm chocolate chip cookies.

Jeanne and Canyon dragged their bags up the gang-plank with a smile on their faces, but inside they felt like two thwarted pirates being asked to jump overboard. Jeanne knew it was four and a half hours before the next plane left for Milwaukee. *Oh well, we can just take a long nap in the gate area*, she thought optimistically.

By 11:00 AM Jeanne and Canyon knew one thing. The person who designed those airport seats had never, ever been stranded in an airport for hours after having had no sleep the night before. No matter what position they tried, the metal arm rests between each seat made it physically impossible to relax enough even to *think* of taking a nap. Instead of sleeping, they read and people-watched.

When final boarding was announced for the 11:30 flight and their names were not called, Jeanne felt a wave of nausea and hunger wash over her. The 3:55 PM flight was next. Four and a half more hours of waiting. Because their finances were extremely tight, she and Canyon split a bag of M & M's and a grease-bomb cheeseburger. By 2:00 PM people-watching had lost its charm.

The airport swarmed with humanity that weekend before Christmas. It reminded Jeanne of what Ellis Island must have been like in the nineteenth century. She felt like a poor, tired, hungry immigrant who was told to wait in another line for four more hours. She started to hate the whole Christmas season.

After the 3:55 flight left at 4:30 PM and nobody at the gate podium even glanced their way, even though Canyon had been up there a number of times to make sure the airline personnel knew they were still waiting to get on, Jeanne contemplated getting on a bus and heading back to Connecticut. She paced. She sat. She watched. She fumed.

An hour later she lost it. "To heck with Christmas! This isn't worth it!" she complained to Canyon. "Let's get out of here!"

He wasn't listening. Mr. "I Can Strike Up a Conversation with Anybody" was chitchatting with a couple who had arrived early for the last flight of the day, the do-or-die 7:30 PM dinner flight.

An announcement came over the intercom. "Ladies

and gentlemen, we're experiencing an overbooking situation and need volunteers to give up their seats until the flight tomorrow morning in exchange for a free ticket to any of the twenty-five cities Midwest Express serves."

The man Canyon was talking to suddenly excused himself and leap-frogged over people to get to the podium. "We can give you three seats," he said. "My wife, daughter and I live in Manhattan, and we can easily get back here tomorrow morning in exchange for free tickets." The gate agent thanked the man and proceeded to fill out his vouchers. Jeanne wanted to scream. There certainly wouldn't be any standbys on *that* flight.

Jeanne was ready for a fight. When the man returned, she glared at Canyon, wishing he'd stop talking to the couple and their daughter. Jeanne was starving. Her head hurt, her back ached, her sinuses felt as if they were ready to implode after breathing all that bad airport air, and she hadn't had any sleep for more than thirty-six hours. She stood up and wondered if smoke was actually coming out of her ears.

That's when she heard Canyon say, "Why sure, we'd love to."

"Love to what?" Jeanne asked bitterly.

"Mr. and Mrs. Caffrey have invited us to spend the night in their Manhattan apartment with them."

Jeanne glared at Canyon. Was he nuts? Stay with complete strangers in their apartment? In New York City? They could be serial killers! Drug dealers! She plopped down in the seat next to the couple who were still chatting with Canyon, dumbfounded that he would even consider such a thing.

Canyon had told them about his job at the hospital and Jeanne's graduate work in art at Yale, and learned that Mr. Caffrey was a psychologist and his daughter was a college student, studying art history. Jeanne was simply too tired to care and didn't offer much to the conversation. The man's wife, Esperanza, originally from Colombia, smiled a lot and spoke with a Spanish accent. All Jeanne wanted to do was sleep.

"We can take the bus back to Manhattan, then catch a bite to eat at our favorite restaurant. You both can use a good night's sleep and a shower, I'm sure." Mr. Caffrey's offer was starting to sound like a dream come true. In a trance, Jeanne gathered her bags and blindly followed Canyon and the family out the door of the airport.

After insisting that they buy Jeanne and Canyon's dinner, Jeanne said her first prayer in days. *Oh, thank You, God. Bless these people whoever they are. And please don't let them mug us when we get to their apartment.* She knew they'd need what little cash they had to get back to the airport the next day and to buy breakfast and possibly lunch. They already knew the first flight the next morning was booked solid, but there was hope they'd make it on the second or third flight of the day. The longer they had to be at the airport eating that expensive snack bar food, the sooner their money would be gone.

When Jeanne and Canyon and the Caffreys arrived at the Manhattan apartment, they looked at each other nervously. The elevator doors opened and Esperanza said something to her husband in Spanish as she hurried down the hallway. In a moment they were ushered into their apartment just as the room lit up with hundreds of tiny white Christmas lights. A beautiful Christmas tree sparkled, as did the boughs of evergreen on the fireplace mantle. What a glorious home, decorated so festively for the holidays! Suddenly it felt like Christmas.

Mrs. Caffrey smiled and handed them clean sheets, pillows and fresh towels. She showed them the kitchen, bath and the rest of the apartment. "Please, please, make yourselves at home," she implored.

Mr. Caffrey spoke. "We'll be leaving early tomorrow morning. We're booked on the first flight to Milwaukee. You might as well sleep in and get to the airport for the eleven-thirty flight. Help yourself to food in the kitchen, and when you leave just give the apartment key to the doorman." And with that Mr. Caffrey shook their hands and went to bed.

Jeanne looked at Canyon, too stunned to speak. After a long, hot shower, she fell asleep on the Caffreys' comfortable living room sofa. The next morning Jeanne and Canyon ate a light breakfast, picked up the apartment, wrote the Caffreys a thank-you note, and left for the airport.

Even though they didn't get on any of the flights that day and had to spend the next night on the floor of the airport, they did make it to Milwaukee on the first flight Monday morning. Somehow, that whole next day and night at LaGuardia passed by, not just in a blur of people-watching, reading and talking . . . but mostly thinking about the Caffreys and their amazing gift of Christmas hospitality.

Thanks to Mr. and Mrs. Caffrey, Jeanne Lorenz learned that Christmas is about struggle. It's about what it's like to have no room at the inn, to be turned away time and time again as they were at that airline gate. She learned that Christmas is not only a celebration of giving, it's a celebration of friendship, no matter how new that friendship is. It's about learning to accept gifts from strangers when we're in need and about giving others a chance to give. She learned that, especially at Christmas, life's too short to play it safe.

Chapter Three

Freedom Hoo-has

Why get your underwear all knotted up into a bunch over things you don't enjoy doing in the first place? Hate housework? Hire a housekeeper! Can't afford it? Barter with him or her for something you do like to do. Fill her freezer with casseroles or watch his children or do her mending. Trade away all the things you don't like to do in life for those things you love.

Freedom means feeling good about who you are and what you do. It's a simple concept. We all have talents or things we're good at. If we share our talents with others and let others share theirs with us, whoa, what a concept! It's just about the best formula in the world. Remember, freedom begets happiness. And life is simply too short not to be happy.

Life's Too Short
to Worry about
Getting Old

FOR THOSE OF YOU in your twenties, thirties or forties, busy raising your families and thinking you've got the world by the tail, in spite of the fact that you've never been busier in your life ... I've got good news for you. Life gets better, lots better. I have recently come to the conclusion that the fifties may be the best decade of all. Having been a single parent since 1985, I'm finally getting the hang of it and I'm even starting to like my singleness now that I'm in my fifties.

The best news is I also know people in their sixties, seventies and eighties who are so vibrant and alive that they could single-handedly be a lobbyist on the national level for the good life. And, of course, they think the sixties, seventies or eighties are the best decades of life.

But back to what I know best: life in the fifties. Married or single, we half-century-old folks can have the world by the tail if we want to. It just takes a little planning.

Start in your twenties and don't buy stuff. Instead, make double or triple house payments so you can pay off the beast in ten or fifteen years instead of twenty-five or thirty, thus saving yourself a hundred grand or more in interest payments. I paid off my thirty-year house loan in seven years while living like a pauper. But I saved something like one hundred and eighty thousand dollars in interest on a house that's worth less than that.

In short, if you save now, you can spend later. You don't need stuff when you're young. You've got enough in your life just keeping up with Little League, soccer, music lessons, sports events, civic organizations, church classes, athletic games, plays, recitals, etc., etc. Save it all for your empty nest when your life isn't quite so busy. In your fifties and beyond, when your kids are grown, you can buy stuff, travel, or just chill out and not have to work so hard . . . translated, you could have a part-time job instead of a fifty-hour-a-week stress-filled nightmare.

It's easy to stop buying stuff. Decide to do it and just do it. I once stopped buying clothes for three years and four months just to see if I could do it. What I learned, while saving tons of money on my wardrobe, is that shopping is a mindless pastime that too many of us pursue like a hobby.

Another way I've saved money in my forties and fifties is by driving the same compact car for years. I bought the car new in 1987, and my loyal preventative maintenance program on "Old Red" has me convinced that my little red wagon will go on and on and on. I hope well past the two-hundred-thousand-mile mark, maybe even three hundred thousand miles, thus saving me untold thousands of dollars on new or even slightly new cars.

Now that I know that I don't need a truckload of money for clothes and cars and other useless stuff, I can, in my fifties and beyond, do what I love best . . . exactly *what* I want to do *when* I want to do it. For me, traveling from sea to shining sea and to countries near and far is my reward for my frugal earlier years.

Another wonderful thing about your fifties is usually most of your children are grown and on their own. The empty nest means the only cooking, cleaning and laundry we have to do is that which is required for ourselves and a spouse if we have one.

When I entered my fifties, I stepped into a whole new wonder-world where my basic philosophy of cooking and cleaning can be summed up in a few choice phrases, which are typed on bright yellow paper and taped to my kitchen cabinets. They include:

Help keep the kitchen clean—eat out.
My next house will have no kitchen,
just vending machines.
A clean house is a sign of a misspent life.
A messy kitchen is a happy kitchen
and this kitchen is delirious.
Countless numbers of people have eaten
in this kitchen and gone on to lead normal lives.
Housework done properly can kill you.
A balanced diet is a cookie in each hand.

Now that my youngest is a full-time college student eighteen hundred miles from home, my life has definitely changed. Now, instead of six loads of laundry a week (How is it that teenagers can manage to get twenty outfits dirty in one week?), I have one hefty load every other week. Now, instead of grocery shopping, planning, cooking and cleaning up the kitchen, I eat out a lot and when I do cook I make enough for six meals. Then I eat two of them and freeze the rest for later cook-free nights. Now, instead of cleaning, dusting, vacuuming, scrubbing and polishing, I give one little talk for forty-five minutes and earn enough money for two or three visits from the cleaning lady. Now, instead of hauling four kids all over kingdom come for their activities, I have the car and time all to myself.

Ah yes, my empty nest is lined with satin, luxurious goose down and stardust. My fifties are fun, fabulous, funny and feisty. To my mind, youth is wasted on young people. Sakes alive, I'll take fifty-five any day. And even sixty-five is starting to look like fun.

Life's Too Short to Put Parents in a Nursing Home

IT WAS TIME FOR PAT to redecorate the bedroom. She had put it off for years, always using the moncy for something else . . . Tom's college tuition, Cathy's braces and nursing school, Jim's diving classes, Michael's trip to Mexico to visit their foreign exchange student.

But now the children were grown, making their way through various post-high-school adventures, all except for Michael, and he would be graduating next year. Yes, it was time to redecorate the bedroom.

First, Pat and her husband Al bought the century-old black walnut bedroom set at an auction in northern Wisconsin. The seven-foot-high headboard, ornate dresser and matching chest of drawers were splendid, especially after they painted the room bright white to show off the beautiful dark wood furniture.

Next, Pat hired a decorator who designed the most magnificent blue and white draperies. Thick pale blue carpet picked up tones from the multicolored sunburst quilt, lovingly made for the couple by their best friends for their twenty-fifth wedding anniversary. The pillows, pictures, knickknack shelf . . . everything was perfect. Elegant yet comfortable. Solid antique treasures mingled with the relaxed playfulness that Pat and Al had been enjoying lately. They both sensed that as their parenting years were ending, it was time now to enjoy life and each other.

Camelot lasted two months. In May, Al's eighty-seven-year-old mother Mabel came to live with them.

It seemed the sensible thing to do. As much as Mabel hated to leave her own home in River Falls, her high blood pressure and kidney trouble made it unsafe for her to live alone. She'd moved into a lovely nursing home a month earlier but each time they visited, Mabel lamented, "I can't stand this place! There's no kitchen! How do they expect me to entertain my friends? I'll come live with you. At least you have a kitchen."

It wasn't a problem for Pat to take in Mabel. As a full-time nurse, head of pediatrics at a hospital near their home, Pat knew that Mabel's medication needed to be better regulated. She figured she could do that easily if they lived together.

Plus, there was the fact that Al's mother had driven the five and a half hours from River Falls to their home in Milwaukee many times over the years to stay with their children when Al and Pat took trips together, and always for weeks at a time when each of the four children was born. Mabel had been Pat's support system, caring for her children, mending their clothes, cooking their meals . . . always there when Pat needed her.

Now Mabel needed them.

The only room large enough for Grandma's treasured pieces of furniture that she insisted on bringing with her was the master bedroom. The newly redecorated master bedroom.

Pat and Al put in a fashionable daybed that converted easily to a comfortable twin. Mabel's favorite chair, desk, lamp, framed pictures, sewing table, and odds and ends from her house were also settled into the room.

That part was easy. The hard part was moving the elegant walnut bedroom set into the small room down the hall . . . the room with the race car wallpaper.

When Grandma arrived, she made it quite clear that the kitchen was her domain. Every day when Al walked the half block from the high school where he was a teacher to their home to have lunch, Grandma fed him soup beefed up with leftovers. Then she'd start peeling potatoes. By the time Pat arrived home from work at 4:30 PM, the potatoes would be boiled and a lettuce and mayonnaise salad cooling in the refrigerator.

"Supper's ready, except for the meat. Didn't know what you had planned" were Mabel's daily words of greeting. Pat started hiding the potatoes.

And cookies. Oh, how Mabel loved to bake cookies. Trouble is she almost always forgot to take them out of the oven in time, so instead of cookies she produced little briquettes. Al would reach for one and Mabel would chuckle, then warn, "Those are dunkers, hard enough to kill a bird." Soon, all of her cookies earned the name *Kill-a-birds*.

That summer was one of ups and downs while the

family learned to adjust. Mabel had to adjust to David and his high-school friends. And to the constant ringing of the phone. She would say, "Must be supper time, phone's ringing again." She had to adjust to the stereo, Al's busy coaching seasons, Pat's long hours at the hospital, the erratic meals and her new environment.

The family had to adjust to Mabel's fierce independence, her memory failures ("I already took my pills!"), her old-fashioned way of cooking and dominance of the kitchen, her increasing urinary problems, and her threats whenever the slightest thing upset her ("I'll get my own apartment!").

In the meantime problems started developing with Pat's mother Olive, also in her eighties, who lived alone in a small farmhouse just fourteen miles from where Mabel had lived in River Falls.

First, Olive developed Parkinson's disease, a neurological disorder, then she fell and broke her hand. A small nursing home was her next stop, but like Mabel she hated it.

"There's no life in this place! I'm all cooped in. Folks here are real nice, but I just can't stand not *doing* anything!"

Pat drove up one weekend in August, checked her mother out of the nursing home for a two-week vacation, brought her back to Milwaukee, and soon realized that both Mabel and Olive belonged in their home. After all, they'd known each other and compared Mother's Day and birthday gifts for twenty-five years, since Al and Pat were married. They'd talked on the phone regularly, Mabel from her elegant city home in River Falls, Olive from her farmhouse outside Ellsworth, comparing news from Pat and Al and the kids.

Yes, Pat thought, *they'll be good for each other here.* Mabel was forgetful, but in pretty good shape physically. Olive was sharp mentally, but confined to a wheelchair. Together they complimented each other, each one doing for the other what the other couldn't do for herself.

So just five months after Pat and Al had redecorated their master bedroom, they had two grannies in their kitchen. The grocery bills skyrocketed as both grandmas' health and eating habits improved. The scheduling problems practically required a computer, but both grandmas thrived on the activity.

Since Al and Pat both left for work early, they hired a woman three days a week to help get both grandmas up, dressed and ready to go to St. Anne's Day Care Center for the Elderly. They arranged for a Care Cab to pick them up and bring them home from the center, where they were treated to a full day of physical and occupational therapy, aerobics and continuing education classes.

The other two days a week they hired Heidi, a young mother with a three-month-old baby, to come in and "sit" with the grandmas. They never figured out who profited more, baby Adam, from all the attention he got from the two grandmas, or the two grandmas, from the youthful antics of Adam and his mama.

All of their lives changed. If Al and Pat wanted to leave at night, they had to make sure Michael was going to be home. If Michael had plans with his friends, more often than not, he'd agree to leave the party or come home temporarily around nine o'clock for "Granny Patrol" as he called it.

Michael would make sure both grandmas made it upstairs and were tucked in for the night. Even at age seventeen he didn't mind Granny Patrol. In fact, he didn't think twice about getting his Grandma Olive from her wheelchair to the commode and back again before he helped her into bed.

When Olive's little house was sold, she insisted they move more of her things into their home. Chests of drawers, books, tables, pictures and ancient mementos of her life on the farm all found their way to Milwaukee.

Mabel followed suit by demanding that at least her treasured collection of Haviland china, all two hundred pieces, be brought in so she could "entertain her friends properly" as she put it. Pat gently reminded her that her close friends were in River Falls, but those dishes retained top priority. Soon Pat had delicate pink and white china all over her house.

Other problems developed as the months ticked by. Mabel lost control of her bladder but refused to wear the necessary protection. She'd wet her clothes, then hide them under the bed or hang them back in the closet, hoping they'd dry by morning so she could wear them again.

Pat felt like a young mother with mounds of laundry. Only she wasn't young. She was tired. Her mother said, "Pat, when you die and get to heaven, I hope they have a washing machine there or else you won't know you're home!"

Both Al's mother and Pat's mother developed arthritis.

Their sewing days were over. Sometimes the pain and inability to use their fine motor skills made them cranky.

Pat's mother, especially, often became depressed and manipulative. "I'm pitiful and such a bother. I'm no good anymore." Al would give her a hug of reassurance and still Olive would say, "I don't know how you can stand it with me here."

Sometimes friction developed between Al and Pat. She would come home from work, tired from a long day in the pediatrics ward, and both grannies would be floundering about in their not-so-large kitchen. Pat would try to get in to organize things and finally shoo them both out of her way. Al would come on the scene with, "Let Mom do it. She's just trying to help."

That help Pat could do without. Cooking had always been her favorite household duty, and now it seemed she was doomed to a life of meat and boiled potato dinners.

The telephone wasn't even her own anymore. She would be out running errands or at work, the phone would ring and Al's mother would answer with "Yes, this is Mrs. Forsythe." Always the message was wrong if, indeed, she remembered to take a message.

Pat wanted it to work. And usually it did, with a great deal of organization and patience. But sometimes when she was really down, the nursing homes in their area seemed mighty tempting.

Pat prayed. She made jokes. She remembered the days when she had four preschoolers and both grandmas were saving her life.

One night, when the frustrations mounted, Pat retreated to the race car wallpaper bedroom and heard Mabel reading her Bible to Olive in the room next door. Mabel was a staunch Methodist; Olive was a strict Roman Catholic from the old country. Here they were, the city mouse and the country mouse, with the one thing they had in common—the Bible. Mabel read her favorite verse, "For God loved the world so much that he gave his only Son so that anyone who believes in him shall not perish but have eternal life" (John 3:16, TLB).

Pat told herself, "If these two exasperating, wonderful women can have such hope for life eternal, then I can certainly have hope for today, tomorrow and next week." She stared at the race cars for a while and promised herself once and for all that she would never send them back to a nursing home.

Pat wasn't able to keep that promise.

Fourteen months after moving in with Pat and Al, Olive had a severe stroke. From that moment she was completely unaware of her surroundings. She required constant care and a tube down her throat for feeding. A nursing home was the only answer.

Two months after that, Al's mother had to be hospitalized because of severe kidney problems. The same day congestive heart failure resulted and she died peacefully.

Two months later Olive died in the nursing home without ever having regained consciousness.

When they came home from Olive's funeral, Pat remembered something Mabel had said to her the day she arrived to live at their home. The phone was ringing, the TV and the stereo were both on, David and his friends were tearing through the house, their daughter Cathy was pulling up outside to spend the weekend to help get Grandma "settled," and the birds in the backyard were tweeting a springtime symphony. Mabel laughed and said, "Pat, there's more life going on here in this house in five minutes than I saw the whole month in that nursing home!"

The weekend after the second funeral, Al and Pat moved their antique walnut bedroom set back into the master bedroom. He painted the room white again and she painted Early American red and blue stencils along the ceiling border. On the shelf by the bed was a picture of Mabel and Olive sitting together holding hands.

"Somehow," Pat spoke slowly to her husband as they stepped back to admire their work, "this room feels much better now than it did before we had to move out of it. I feel better too. Growing old doesn't seem so scary anymore."

Life's Too Short to Cook

I LIKE TO THINK OF MYSELF as a creative person and, yet, even though my children are musicians, writers and artists, I can't sing, play an instrument, act or draw. But logic says that in order to give birth to such right-brained children, one would have to possess a truckload of creative genes.

Mine emerge in the kitchen.

A normal, less creative person finds an interesting recipe, follows it word for word, line for line, and creates a marvelous culinary masterpiece that's raved about for generations, until his or her name ends up on the recipe as if he or she invented it in the first place.

A truly creative person like me, however, would never think of following a printed recipe word for word. I add, subtract, improvise, create . . . until, *ta-da*, a perfectly good recipe turns to swill.

A truly creative cook like me will add, say, three heaping tablespoons of cocoa to an already tasty oatmeal cookie recipe. Keep in mind that such a deed is simply a response to one's once-every-two-week chocolate craving. Of course, once the cocoa powder was floating on top of the oats and other cookie ingredients, I remembered that unsweetened cocoa is very bitter. And being the creative dieter that I am, I added a couple tablespoons of liquid sweetener, the kind that gives laboratory rats cancer if they look at it, but wouldn't add a slab of fat to my hips the way sugar would . . . which is just another example in my creative solutions bag-o'-tricks.

But then with all that extra liquid *oozing* in the cookie dough, I had to be ultracreative and add something that would soak it up. Coconut. Whatever was left in the bag seemed to be just the right amount. Then I added a cup of walnuts, which were also not in the recipe but had looked at me rather forlornly when I picked up the coconut next to them. Behind the nuts was half a package of milk-chocolate chips. Perfect! After all, I might as well have some real chocolate to bite into when I was eating these creative cookies. And since I'd given up candy for Lent those chocolate-chip, nut, coconut, oatmeal cookies were beginning to sound mighty tasty. Almost like candy bars, in fact! Visions of entering the Pillsbury Bake-Off danced in my head.

I stirred my ingredients thoroughly, but when the time came to "drop by rounded teaspoonfuls" onto the cookie sheet, my recipe didn't want to cooperate. Each glob just sort of crumbled all over the counter. So I grabbed a handful, smashed it together, pounded, rounded, pushed and pulled until I was able to form golf ball-sized masses. I carefully placed them two inches apart on the sheet, knowing that once they hit that 325-degree temperature they'd flatten out into perfectly normal-looking cookies.

Twelve minutes later, when I pulled them out of the

oven, those golf ball-shaped cookies had not flattened one nanomillimeter. Ten minutes later when they'd cooled sufficiently to sample, I carefully picked up an already-named "Rumpled Chocolate Oatmeal Golden Globe." It instantly crumbled into tiny bits. So now what I had, instead of cookies, was crisp, crunchy, chocolate, chocolate-chip, coconut, nut, oatmeal . . . ice cream topping. I'd say that was pretty creative, wouldn't you?

And so it goes. I've been known to add such a variety of things to normal everyday tuna casserole, including last night's leftovers, that my family is aghast at my sense of creativity.

I've also decided that the person who invented cold pasta salad should be canonized. I mean, really, it didn't take me long to figure out that for never-the-same-kind-twice pasta salad, all you have to do is choose one of the dozens of varieties and shapes of pasta, add an unusual medley of vegetables, some sort of protein like meat, eggs, cheese or Spam, and a bottle of any flavor salad dressing.

At potluck dinners, folks are always amazed that I manage to bring, once again, a recipe they haven't heard of. Of course, half the trick is the name you give it . . . like "Spedini-Artichoke-Mozzarella Melangerie."

Creatively deprived people gaze upon me with such adoring looks of awe that I usually leave early so I don't have to be around after they've actually *tasted* my creations. I lose a lot of casserole dishes that way, but it's those initial comments, when the guests first see my unusual-looking concoction, that fill my head with the splendiferous knowledge that I am indeed a creative person. I certainly wouldn't want to press my luck by expecting that my endeavors actually *taste* good.

Tonight's creative delight is a one-dish feast called "Brussels Sprout Turkey à la Greek Star." I'll finally be using that can of salty Greek olives and the jar of baby corn that's been in the back of the cupboard far too long. I plan to make a star-shape on top with the baby corn, dotting each point with a large olive. I'll probably add a cup or so of that alphabet pasta that often adds zing to my extra-creative homemade soups. Once again, it'll be a masterpiece. *Wonder if the dog will like this one? Oh, that's right. We don't have a dog.*

Now that you know my secrets to cooking, I have to admit that my basic philosophy is this: Why make such a big deal about cooking when everybody's just going to eat it all up in fifteen minutes anyway? Cooking, unfortunately, is one of those household chores that must be done every day. Every person on earth eats two, three or, if you have teenagers, nine times a day. In spite of the culinary temptations mentioned above, I am not domestically gifted in this area. I do not get any thrills from making little roses out of radishes. I never have, nor will I ever, surprise my family with a flaming torte. Stuffed mushrooms with crabmeat-and-ten-other-gooey-ingredients filling? Get real.

Now that I have raised four children and will never see fifty again, I can proudly proclaim that I have never once baked a pie crust from scratch and I never intend to. Come to think of it, I don't think I've ever baked a cake from scratch either.

Baking, *schmaking*. Just tell your friends that you hate to bake and at Christmastime you'll be the recipient of plate after plate, box after box of *their* homemade Christmas cookies. So many people I know love to bake cookies so much that they bake enough for the entire armed services. Some people start baking Christmas cookies in September and freeze dozens upon dozens of delightful confections. Then, during the weeks before Christmas, they take pride in creating lovely platefuls of their creative delights for all their nonbaking friends. The critical part is making sure you get on their list of nonbaking friends. The element of pity for your family usually prompts the addition of a dozen or more cookies to the pile. Believe me, we in the Lorenz household have never ever gone cookie-hungry at Christmas, because we make sure everyone knows that I don't bake.

Cooking, in my book, fits in the list of things I don't like to do, somewhere between getting the cobwebs off the ceiling and cleaning out the fireplace. Why slave for hours on petit fours, chocolate mousse or spinach soufflé when it all disappears in a matter of minutes or, once again, seconds, if you have teenagers? Most people will pop a dry Triscuit into their mouth with the same appreciation and verve as they would a cracker topped with anchovy paste over a tiny scalloped-edged fluted cucumber that is then topped with a sliced black olive with a pimiento and a pickled garlic clove sticking proudly out of its center.

Three good chews and it's all gone anyway, so what's the difference? Wouldn't you rather be remembered for the sparkling conversation and exciting guests at your parties than for the fourteen-steps-per-square-inch hors d'oeuvres you slaved over for hours? Of course you would.

If actual cooking and the nightmare of party foods give you hives, take heart. There is a way to avoid cooking. It's called good health.

It's easy. Start talking to your family about the evils of sugar, cholesterol, overcooked food, and anything with preservatives and additives. Bring home everything you can find in the produce department. Wean your family from Twinkies to turnips. From candy to cabbage. From butter cookies to Brussels sprouts. And don't bother peeling those vegetables and fruits, especially if they're organically grown. Tell your family that fiber prevents colon cancer. Tell them that white fish cooked in the microwave is much better for them than a ham-and-potato-and-cheese casserole that takes hours to prepare. It is better for them, so hold your head up high.

Slowly withdraw those homemade, gooey baked goods that turn to flab the minute they come out of the oven or off the bakery store shelves. Forget those overcooked, nonnutritious nourished casseroles and meat-and-potato dinners. Convince your family that yogurt, tofu, bean sprouts and soy nuts are tasty as well as nutritious. Point out that a juicy red apple is a much better dessert than death-by-chocolate, triple chocolate cake. Keep at them until they, too, believe that your main motive is the health and well-being of your family. You're the only one who has to know that healthy eating means less cooking.

Take heart. Your kids will probably forgive you for this good health campaign by the time they're in their sixties and seventies and the workings of their colon are part of normal conversation.

Life's Too Short to Collect Stuff

OVER THE YEARS I've collected all sorts of things: unusual napkin rings, antique hat pins, beach glass, old crocks, glassware, rag rugs, brass and silver. But a few years ago I noticed a heavy feeling whenever I looked at my collections. I wasn't sure why, but the fun had gone out of collecting.

Why do I have so many things? I thought to myself.

Then, surprisingly, I answered right back, *They're your treasures, keepsakes, things to pass on to your children and grandchildren. Besides, they're fun to look at and display.*

Then something happened in 1993 that made me see my collections in a whole different light. I was in Louisville, Kentucky, visiting my brother and sister-in-law. One day we attended an auction . . . a little slice of heaven for a collector like me. The newspaper ad proclaimed it to be "The Lifetime Collection of Donald and Janet Dixon."

I wondered if Mr. and Mrs. Dixon were paring down their possessions before moving into a retirement home. I wondered if perhaps one of them had died recently.

What my brother, sister-in-law and I discovered when we pulled into the driveway was that Donald and Janet Dixon were millionaires. Their house, on acres and acres of a perfectly manicured estate, complete with a huge in-ground pool and Jacuzzi, had sold to the first looker for six hundred and fifty thousand dollars. All of their exquisite possessions were sitting on the front lawn under huge tents, waiting to be sold. More than four hundred items worth hundreds of thousands of dollars were cataloged on legal-sized sheets given to each of the many potential bidders on that hot June afternoon.

Items on the list included: a highly carved Chippendale mahogany king size four post canopy bed on claw feet; superb Queen Anne burl walnut bookcase china cabinet with beveled glass doors, dated 1890; mother of pearl inlaid rosewood tea caddy with hinged box interior, circa 1850; rare signed Tiffany and Company coffee urn; three-piece Ansonia marble clock set with open encasement and mercury pendulum, circa 1880.

This wasn't your typical auction. It also included a Mercedes Benz automobile in superb condition, a six-month-old snazzy red pick-up truck and an Audi 200 Quattro Turbo with heated seats. The Dixons were selling everything, including the wheels right out from under themselves.

"Why would anyone part with all their treasures?" I asked my sister-in-law. Linda just shrugged her shoulders, obviously as mystified as I, and said, "Look at the china, candelabra and cut glass. Think of the parties these people had!"

I ran my fingers over the fine sharp edges of half a dozen huge cut glass vases and umbrella stands. As I walked around a dozen antique Persian rugs stretched out on the lawn, I tried to imagine why or how one could part with such exquisite beauty.

The auction began under another giant tent filled with folding chairs out on the south lawn. The Dixons' pristine navy blue leather sofa sold to the highest bidder for just under two thousand dollars. The huge mahogany dining room table sold for one thousand five hundred dollars. The twelve matching chairs went for $265 each. This definitely wasn't a sale for faint-of-pocketbook folks like myself.

Why? I wondered over and over. *Why would they sell it all? Don't they have children who would want these treasures?* Certainly many of the antique items had been in their families for generations.

We left after three hours, before a third of the items had been sold. My brother managed to outbid the antique dealers and got a dandy oak workbench for fifty dollars. The next day when we went back to the Dixons' with his van to pick up the workbench, my curiosity got the best of me. I just had to know why Donald and Janet Dixon were selling their home and all those exquisite furnishings, antiques and treasures.

When I rang the doorbell, a pretty young woman with long, light brown wavy hair, no makeup and simple clothes answered. *Wow, they even have a maid!* I thought to myself wistfully.

"Is Mrs. Dixon home?" I asked.

"I'm Mrs. Dixon," she said simply, flashing a warm smile.

"Oh my goodness," I stammered. "Forgive me, I don't

mean to intrude but, well, I'm here with my brother. He's out in the garage loading the workbench he bought yesterday. I just had to meet you. I'm wondering if you would mind telling me why you sold all your beautiful possessions."

Mrs. Dixon graciously invited me into their home and introduced me to her husband, who reminded Janet that they had to be at the house closing in forty-five minutes.

I repeated my question to Mr. Dixon. "How could you sell all your beautiful treasures?"

Mr. Dixon, a very good-looking, curly-haired man in his early forties, smiled, put his arm around his wife's waist and said quietly, "Oh, I didn't sell my treasures. All that is just *stuff*. My treasures are right here, my wife and daughter. Have you met our daughter Collyn? She's eleven. Yes, these are my treasures, Janet and Collyn. They are all I need."

Mrs. Dixon explained that the previous April she had gone to the Bahamas for a week with a friend and fallen in love with a tiny island called Green Turtle Cay in Abaco. She called her husband and asked him to join her, so he could see the beauty of the tiny island. Donald flew over the next day, and together they explored the island, befriended the local folks and thoroughly relaxed in a world that had missed out on the twentieth century. After a few days, Janet and Donald decided to change their lives. They agreed to sell their home and all their possessions, and move to the Bahamas with nothing but their bathing suits and a few small personal items.

Janet's eyes danced with excitement as she explained further. "We're leaving tonight. Can you believe it?

Tomorrow our address will be Green Turtle Cay. We're moving into an old, simple, one-story oceanside home with four rooms: a kitchen, living room and two bedrooms. No phone or TV. In fact, there are only two pay phones on the whole island. It takes three weeks for mail to get from here to there.

"We're really looking forward just to spending time together. This life here, these things, the big house, all those furnishings and stuff, the Junior League, it's not me. I don't like what happens to your life when you have money. Things somehow become more important than people. This house and all those expensive items are not important. What's really important is family, sunshine, wind and the sea, and those will be the things we'll have every day on the island."

It was time for me to leave and let the Dixons get on with their lives. I shook hands with Janet and Donald and wished them a happy life. I left with a sense of awe, knowing these wonderful people had given me a valuable gift.

I came home from Louisville and started cleaning house. I gathered up hundreds of items for a rummage sale. I wrapped up a cherished silver casserole dish and two collectible green vases that my sister-in-law had admired, and shipped them off to her.

I gift-wrapped a set of antique butter plates that had been in my family for three generations and gave them to a neighbor couple who had just gotten married. I gave my brass collection to my son for Christmas. I placed 150 books on my dining room table and insisted that friends in my women's group each take a handful of them home. I gave most of my silver collection to my four children. The next spring I put more than one hundred items on a big table out by the street in front of my house with a huge sign that simply said FREE. Every month I try to clean out one closet or one drawer full of stuff, and either give it away or toss it.

Giving away my things slowly but deliberately is giving me a sense of freedom, a cleansing of sorts. It's fun to see how much the people who receive my things are enjoying them as much as I did.

But the best part is now that I've stopped collecting things and started giving them away, I have less clutter around the house to dust, which means I have more time to spend with family and friends. And they, as the Dixons taught me, are my real treasures.

Life's Too Short
to Get Knotted Up
over Housework

HOUSEWORK IS A NEMESIS. A plague. Something akin to chicken pox—many folks go through it but nobody likes it.

Oh, I've tried to clean my house. Even read books on how to do it more efficiently. But there's something about it that causes my brain automatically to think of fifty other things that sound like more fun than housework.

I've hated housework for more than forty years, ever since I was a little kid and my mother taught me how to clean the bathroom, vacuum, dust, and pick up after my little brother and sister. Since then, I've complained about it, put it off, apologized for not doing it and often wished I had a full-time, live-in housekeeper. But, alas, that dream will undoubtedly never come true.

Over the years I've discovered that even in the Bible people had their share of cleaning problems. In fact, many verses explain the way I feel about housework. For instance, right in the beginning, in Genesis 31:40–41 (TLB) it says, "I worked for you through the scorching heat of the day, and through the cold and sleepless nights. Yes, twenty years . . . ! And you have reduced my wages ten times!" I figure that wage-reducing part applies to me because we housework-doers not only don't get any wages at all, we're actually falling into the red because we don't get cost-of-living increases.

Since men are much more domesticated these days, I'm sure there are those who hate housework just as much as I do. I hope that my biblical research will help men and women alike take comfort in the fact that this housework nemesis is an age-old problem.

The Bible offers descriptions of household messes created by our forefathers that are a homemaker's nightmare. In Exodus 29:36 (TLB) it says, "Every day you shall sacrifice a young bull as a sin offering for atonement; afterwards, purge the altar by making atonement for it; pour olive oil upon it to sanctify it." Have you ever tried to clean up spilled olive oil? First you wipe up as much as you can with paper towels. Then you wash with a soapy solution, then you rinse. We're talking major work here. And just thinking about the mess made by sacrificing bulls, lambs and rams gives me the shivers.

In the early 1980s, when I had a husband and four children all living at home, I agreed to cosign with my husband on a loan for a house with three bathrooms. Three! Having lived in one-bathroom houses all my life, it was a shock, let me tell you. How would a woman who hates to clean anything survive cleaning three bathrooms? But then I remembered that three of my children were old enough to wield a rag and a mop. And since they all liked to use the bathroom every now and then—say five to six hours a day considering that they were all preteens whose best friends were mirrors—I figured I had three built-in bathroom cleaners. So I signed on the dotted line and bought the house.

After that, every Tuesday was bathroom cleaning day. One kid per bathroom and thirty minutes later, the mingled scent of Comet, Vanish and Fantastik wafted through the entire house with more punch than if Mr. Clean himself had stopped in. Trouble is, one by one, in a four-year span, the three older kids departed for college never to return . . . except for visits now, when they expect every bathroom to be a shining example of their former selves.

I tell you, it's depressing. But once again I turned to the Good Book, and my heart was gladdened. Glad mainly because I don't live in the days of Isaiah. I guess they were pretty lousy housekeepers back then. In Isaiah 28:7–8 (TLB) it says, "Jerusalem is now led by drunks! Her priests and prophets reel and stagger, making stupid errors and mistakes. Their tables are covered with vomit; filth is everywhere." *Well now*, I think to myself as I grab my aerosol cans and spray bottles, *just be glad you don't have to clean that up!* See how uplifting the Bible is?

My laundry days were lightened considerably after I read the book of Job. Job was a frustrated man, a man who struggled with the notion that he might never learn how to be good enough for God's approval. Job understood God's wrath. In Job 9:30–31 (TLB) he cries out, "Even if I were to wash myself with purest water and cleanse my hands with lye to make them utterly clean, even so you would plunge me into the ditch and mud; and even my clothing would be less filthy than you consider me to be!" I know how poor Job feels. I once tried to clean the clothes of a kid who fell into a muddy ditch. Talk about gut-wrenching hopelessness.

Housework's the same. Why go to the trouble when the kids are going to be home from school any minute and just mess it all up again?

We home dwellers all know the worst job of all is washing windows. During the first dozen years of my married life, I lived in three apartments and three houses. Quite honestly, before I moved into my present home, I only washed the windows in each dwelling once. After that initial grueling push 'em up, pull 'em down, screens off, screens on, storms up, storms down and do-it-all-again-from-the-inside routine, I would wait two, sometimes three years and then move. Once I moved from Denver to St. Louis, just to make sure none of the neighbors would recognize me as the lady with those awful windows.

When I think about washing windows, I get dreamy-eyed and find myself wishing I had lived in biblical times. After all, glass hadn't been invented yet and nobody ever had to wash windows. A few tent flaps, maybe, but no windows.

If you think moving is a drastic measure for evading housework, it's nothing compared to another of my housework-evading schemes. First my oven became so dirty that whenever I turned it on, the burning odors from the food residue kept setting off the smoke alarm. The second thing was that I inherited a cat. Cleaning the cat's litter box was a chore that sent chills up my spine. I was "grossed out" before being "grossed out" was even popular.

Shortly after the cat joined the family, I read an article that said pregnant women should not clean litter boxes. I also remembered reading that pregnant women should not use oven cleaner. I thought to myself, *Nine whole months of not having to clean the litter box or the oven?* I called my husband into the bedroom, and we had a nice long talk that night. Well, not *that* much talk.

If cleaning certain things around your house is a pet peeve of monstrous proportions, as my oven and litter box were for me, take heart. Just be glad you're not living back in the days of King Ahab in the Old Testament. In I Kings 22:38 (TLB), just after King Ahab's death, we learn that his body was taken to Samaria and buried there. "When his chariot and armor were washed beside the pool of Samaria, where the prostitutes bathed, dogs came and licked the king's blood just as the Lord had said would happen." Personally I prefer a hose and a bucket of clean suds when I clean my chariot. Actually, I really prefer the drive-through, three-minute car wash located five minutes from my house.

Once you've given up housework, think of all the extra time you're going to have. Why, you can find new hobbies, travel, read more, go back to school or get an extra job, and use the money to buy the latest computerized, do-it-all combo microwave, dishwasher, washer/dryer. Your housework days will practically be over!

Or, better yet, hire a cleaning service to come in once a month to do the vacuuming and dusting. In short, if you truly hate to clean as I do, get a job and pay someone else to do what you hate. Remember, life's too short to get your shorts all wadded into a ball over housework.

We need to admit that housecleaning is a bugaboo that's going to leave many of us wilted, defeated and depressed for generations to come. At least we can take heart that things weren't much easier in biblical times. At the end of my favorite Psalm 91:16 (TLB) it says, "I will satisfy him with a full life and give him my salvation." I just hope on the day of judgment the good Lord doesn't stumble over my dust bunnies, get grossed out when He tries to look through my windows, or be distracted by any grime, grease or grossness emanating from my happy but somewhat dusty I-hate-housework home. After all, we just get graded on what's in our hearts. Don't we?

Chapter Four

Scrapbook Adventures

I have a Benjamin Franklin quote laminated and taped to the front of my computer. It says, "Write things worth reading or do things worth writing." I'll probably never sign my name on a multimillion-dollar contract to write a best-selling novel. It's just not me. I know my limitations. But, do things worth writing? Absolutely! In order to have adventures worth writing about, I had to adopt a new philosophy. And this is it: Never say no to an opportunity unless it's illegal or immoral. That philosophy has taken me all over the United States of America, including Hawaii for my fiftieth birthday; to Japan, Singapore and Malaysia to attend the wedding of a woman I'd only met once, and to six European countries flying standby with inexpensive passes. When you say yes to an opportunity, the adventures that crop into your life become the thread in the fabric of who you are. And the friends you meet and make along the way are the satin bindings on that quilt of life.

Life's Too Short
to Sit on the Shore

I WAS DEFINITELY NOT looking forward to my fiftieth birthday until my oldest daughter Jeanne called from California.

"Mom, you're supposed to do 'Hawaii Five-oh' when you turn fifty. It's a tradition. I'll pay your airfare. I'm taking you to Hawaii next summer for your birthday."

The day before my fifteen-year-old son Andrew and I left to join Jeanne and her boyfriend Canyon on our adventure of a lifetime, I received a letter from Social Security.

"I don't understand this," I blubbered to the representative on the phone after I tore open the letter.

She responded kindly, "If a minor child only has one living parent, that parent receives financial help from Social Security until the child is sixteen. The child continues to receive it until he's eighteen, however."

I hung up the phone in a daze. In four months, my Social Security payments—one-third of my annual income—would be gone.

Well, it was too late to cancel the vacation. Jeanne was eagerly awaiting our arrival in California. And besides, I'd saved like the dickens for six months to pay for Andrew's airfare and the rest of the trip. So instead of worrying about the future, I repeated my favorite Bible verse over and over: "Commit thy way unto the Lord; trust also in him; and he shall bring it to pass" (Psalm 37:5, KJV).

The vacation was spectacular, but when I returned home and started thinking about how my financial future was in a downward spiral, my approaching-fifty body decided to have its own heyday.

First, a huge portion of my back tooth broke into little pieces. When the crown was put in, I had to fork out $487 to my dentist. No dental insurance, of course.

The next day I received a bill for X-rays of my arthritic toe, which I'd had before the trip . . . $144. The meager medical insurance I could afford didn't cover X-rays.

That same week I noticed I was having trouble reading the fine print and sometimes even the medium print. Out of desperation I purchased a huge light for the kitchen that contained four fluorescent bulbs, each four feet long. It made cooking, bill paying, reading and letter writing at the kitchen counter much easier for my approaching-fifty eyes. But that new light set me back $107.

Next I made a trip to the optometrist's office. He said both my distance and close-up vision were worse.

Naturally, I thought bitterly, as my whole physical well-being flashed before my eyes in bright neon. It said, *You're almost fifty. Over the hill.*

The bill for the new bifocals and reading glasses was $241.

That same week, I finally gave in to one too many backaches caused by the ancient desk chair in my home office. I figured that the lower back pain was just another old age pitfall.

But once again, I repeated my favorite verse from Psalms, acted on faith, and wrote out a check for $105 for a superb office chair with arms and lumbar support. The day after I put that chair together, I noticed a great improvement in my back.

Well, now, at least my broken tooth was fixed, I could see near and far with my new glasses, my back didn't hurt, and my arthritic toe felt better after all the hiking I did in Hawaii. Physically, things seemed to be looking up. But financially, things were out of control. First my income was going down by a third, then all those bills. I wasn't just going over the hill agewise, I was careening downhill financially too.

And so I prayed. "Thank You, Lord, for providing for my son and me." Of course, I ended the prayer with Psalm 37:5. I firmly believed that if I truly trusted the Lord, I had to do just that . . . trust Him to take care of us. But I still wasn't happy about turning fifty.

The next week as I started putting my photo album together from the trip to Hawaii, I recalled the most exciting day we'd had on the big island.

On the morning of day twelve, we rented ocean kayaks and paddled a mile or so to the most spectacular snorkeling spot. The Technicolor fish and amazing coral filled our underwater day with awe. Late in the afternoon as we started back across the bay to return the rented kayaks, we lollygagged across the calm, crystal clear ocean water.

Suddenly dolphins were popping out of the water just ahead of us! Dozens of them, at least eighty or one hundred. We paddled like crazy to get closer, then the four of us sat in silence when we reached the spot where the dolphins were playing. As we sat motionless in that great ocean, those dolphins jumped out of the water, did spins and flips in the air, dove in perfect unison, and entertained us all around our two kayaks. They seemed as happy to see us as we were to see them, and for twenty minutes we were spellbound.

Canyon spoke first, almost in a whisper. "This is a God moment. I'll never forget this as long as I live."

I nodded as six sleek dolphins, in perfect synchronization, jumped out of the water, then glided within feet of the kayak Andrew and I were in.

As I tucked photos of Hawaiian beaches, sunsets and volcanoes into my album, I thought about what Canyon had said.

A God moment, I mused. Perhaps my life at this junction of turning fifty is a God moment. Could it be that turning fifty means a new freedom, a chance to swim and dance and spin with the same glee and abandonment that the dolphins had demonstrated?

It's true, I thought, *those magnificent creatures had plenty of worries of their own, like where the next couple hundred fish would come from for dinner that night, and how to protect their young from sharks and other predators. And yet there they were playing and entertaining us with complete, joyful abandonment in the environment that God had provided.*

Unknowingly, those dolphins had committed their way to the Lord and were enjoying their very existence to the fullest. Why couldn't I do the same?

Right then I decided to "work smarter" a few extra hours in my home office each day until I could get all those medical bills paid off.

I made a promise to myself not to buy any clothing or unneeded household items for three years. After all, I had plenty of clothes and if I just stayed out of the stores, I'd resist impulse buying.

Next, I made a list of all the things I could do with my life after Andrew, my youngest, went to college. I could teach workshops in various parts of the country. Write books. Visit more friends and relatives. Sleep longer in the mornings. Stay up later at night. Eat when I feel like it. Take more bike rides. Make new friends.

Suddenly I felt as free as one of those dolphins in the balmy Pacific Ocean. My faith tells me that the Lord does take care of all His creatures, great and small, dolphins and damsels. And whether I'm thirty, fifty or ninety, there's plenty waiting for me on the horizon, no matter what decade I'm in.

Life's Too Short
to Say No to an
Opportunity

WE ALL KNOW PEOPLE who never seem to have any grand travel adventures because they can't bring themselves to break their routine.

They always come up with excuses when you suggest something different or exciting to do. Years ago, to avoid that safe, comfortable road myself, I took on a philosophy of life that says, "Never say no to an opportunity unless it's illegal or immoral."

Believe me, that one sentence has handed me more than my share of adventures. One of my favorites began in 1996, when I received a delightful letter from a woman named Winnie Chai in Kuala Lumpur, Malaysia. She'd read a story I wrote that touched her. Full-blooded Chinese, her parents had migrated from China to Malaysia in the late 1940s. Her parents were devout Catholics, and she was educated by nuns in Malaysia and taught to speak perfect English. Winnie is seven years younger than I am, had never been married but longed to have a family of her own.

I was so taken by her letter that I wrote her back. I told her all about my four children, my single-parent stresses and my life in America. After that we started writing regularly via e-mail.

A year later I got a phone call. "Pat, I'm in New York! First time I've ever been to the United States, and I just wanted to hear your voice." Winnie worked for Panasonic in Malaysia and was visiting colleagues in the states. I convinced her that she needed to see another part of America, and invited her to fly to Wisconsin and spend a few days with me.

Winnie arrived the next morning. We spent four days seeing the sights and getting to know each other. After she left, we continued e-mailing off and on for the next two years until August 1999, when I received a note that said, "Pat, Chris has asked me to marry him! The wedding is September 25 and you must come. Please try to make it."

Because of my philosophy about never saying no to an opportunity and knowing I could fly standby for pennies on the dollar because my sister-in-law worked for a major airline, I said, "Of course! Yes, I'll come!"

At the time I didn't have a clue as to what the trip involved, but I soon found out. The morning of Sunday, September 19, 1999, I took the 7:30 airport bus from Milwaukee to Chicago's O'Hare Airport, waited two hours, boarded a jumbo jet, flew twelve hours to Japan, waited there for three hours, boarded another plane for a six-hour flight to Singapore, was met there at midnight (which was really 9:00 AM my time) by an Indian friend of Winnie's named Sreela who took me to her uncle's house to spend the night. The next morning Sreela's uncle put us on the bus to Kuala Lumpur, another six-hour adventure. Finally at 3:00 PM Tuesday we arrived in Kuala Lumpur, spent time at Sreela's house and at six o'clock Tuesday evening finally met up with Winnie at the church in time for choir rehearsal for the wedding.

Because the bride was busy with last-minute preparations, I spent the next three days either sightseeing on guided tours by myself or with a variety of Winnie's amazingly wonderful friends. On my own I visited museums, the king's palace, an art festival, a park with a sculpture garden, a scorpion factory, a batik factory and a pewter factory. Sreela took me to Little India and out for the most marvelous tea in the world at her favorite coffeehouse.

Nilo—another of Winnie's friends who shared the small floor of the living room with me as our bed-away-from-home—and I toured Chinatown and the Central Market, and attended the four separate events of the wedding day. Nilo, an Indian Muslim raised in Malaysia, is married to an Englishman and has lived in London for the past ten years. We became such good friends in those days before and during the wedding that we're both planning visits to each other's homes and have become e-mailing buddies.

In ten days I traveled over twenty thousand miles by air, bus and car. I met dozens upon dozens of incredibly open, friendly people, ate either Malaysian, Chinese or Indian food at every meal, climbed 364 steps in the rain to see the inside of the Temple Cave (and 364 steps down!), used bathrooms that were more primitive than outhouses, as well as elegant bathrooms that put our Western ones to shame. I visited my new Malaysian and Singaporian friends in four different homes and saw four different lifestyles up close and personal. I had long, late-evening talks about what's important in life, and I was part of the most amazing wedding.

That week I met people from India, China, Japan and England who'd come in for the big wedding. Winnie's mother (who is Chinese and doesn't speak English) and I communicated with hand motions, pidgin English, and lots of smiles. She told Winnie it was like a duck talking to a goose, but somehow we managed to communicate.

After the morning wedding we were treated to an Asian lunch and then witnessed the formal, traditional Japanese tea ceremony. That evening hundreds of guests at the reception were treated to an eight-course Chinese dinner at a five-star hotel. After dinner I joined the dancing in the two long lines of folks so diverse in their ethnic back grounds that it looked like a gathering of the United Nations.

Is there an opportunity staring at you today? Say, *Yes!* You'll never know where that opportunity might take you or how it might change your life.

Life's Too Short to Stay Home

IT WAS HIS IDEA. A family vacation. Seven days alto-gether and, boy, did he mean *all together*. Two days get-ting there. Two days back. Three days of actual vacation in the land of the sun. We'd drive, he insisted. Cheaper that way.

I didn't like the way those numbers stacked up. But who was I to put a crimp in the family vacation? Besides, after seven months of winter cold in Wisconsin, three days of sunshine on the Gulf of Mexico outside Tallahassee, Florida, sounded rather glorious. Even if we did have to take the kids. Even if we did have to go in July.

Some friends owned a second home on the Gulf and insisted that we stay there during our Southern interlude. They said, "Come anytime! The key is under the middle flower pot in the window box on the front of the house."

If you want to know the truth, I really wasn't too crazy about this vacation at all, right from the beginning. My husband and I had never gone more than a hundred miles in a car without a petty argument or a heady discussion turning into a major nobody-talks-to-anybody blow-up. Mix that little personality nuance with four children rang-ing in ages from sixteen down to two and you have the basic ingredients for a mass-murder-suicide or at least a trip to a marriage counselor.

I was convinced that there was not a car, van or motor home big enough to hold six struggling individuals for four days. He insisted we take our midsize sedan. The one with the hump in the back seat.

I packed light. Just enough shorts, T-shirts and swim-suits for me and the four kids to scrape by on. He loaded the trunk with a five-gallon cooler, two lawn chairs, a plas-tic raft, swim fins, snorkel, fishing gear, golf clubs, his three-piece summer suit and enough clothes for a three-week stint in Maui.

I took sensible car snacks: apples, small cans of fruit juice and carsick pills. He threw chocolate bars, bubble gum, potato chips and malted milk balls on the dashboard.

Shortly after dawn's early light on the morning of blastoff, I placed the two-year-old securely in his required safety seat in the front between me and the Vacation Wizard. The other three kids raced for the two windows in the back seat. "Legs," the sixteen-year-old who took les-sons on growing from Wilt the Stilt, lost the contest and started yelling about how the hump in the middle was crushing his tailbone.

The eleven-year-old announced that she was going to navigate. The pilot agreed and tossed her a handful of maps. He said she was on her own and that she better keep us going south or else.

After forty-five minutes on the highway, the Map Reader told us the interstate we were on didn't go south at all. She insisted we were on an east-west toll. I reached for my heart pills and vowed not to start any arguments during this vacation. Then I remembered, I don't take heart pills.

After a colossal argument between Map Reader and Legs about road signs and interstates and toll roads and following directions, the prepubescent creature next to the window admitted the error of her ways with a loud *"Hurrummmppph,"* a side punch to her brother's ribs and began what turned out to be a full-blown, two-hour pout.

Meanwhile, the two-year-old lurched forward and miraculously captured the malted milk ball bag off the dashboard. I was tying the shoe of the whiny, thirsty five-year-old sitting behind me. Before I even knew what had happened, Wee One had bitten through the package and scattered malted milk balls all over the front seat, into my purse and onto the floor. As you can imagine, malted milk balls, when lodged near one's thighs in a car that by now was registering ninety-six degrees because the air-conditioning system had not been given the benefit of a Freon check for more than five years (I learned later from the Vacation Wizard) do not stay firm for long.

The Twirp, as the rest of the family affectionately calls the two-year-old, was shoving those hot little brown gooey balls into his mouth as fast as humanly possible. The sixteen-year-old on the hump demanded his share. Map Reader retreated from her pout long enough to call him a "zit-faced oinker" and the five-year-old said she had to go to the bathroom.

The Vacation Wizard announced there'd be no potty

stops for two hours and would everyone please shut up. That's when he put his hand on the seat, came up with a fist full of chocolate goo, rubbed it on his yellow seersucker pants and shouted words that turned the air inside the car a sort of ominous blue color.

"Do you want me to wet my pants?" squeaked the five-year-old.

From Map Reader, "Did you know that there are ten thousand miles of parks in Florida and that we now have only 984 miles before we get to Tallahassee?"

"If I don't get off this hump, these legs belonging to one ace basketball star and insured by Lloyds of London are going to require amputation, and I will remain a paraplegic burden on your lives for all time!"

The Twirp started chanting, "Drink, drink, drink!"

I closed my eyes and tried to imagine how the beach house was decorated. I tried to remember if the boat would hold six people. How many beds were there? I hadn't seen my friends in Florida for more than fifteen years, but I was sure the accommodations would be plush. Irene had said, "Our house is your house."

I awoke from my daydream when the family sedan started hobbling precariously on three wheels. The Vacation Wizard managed to bring the thump-thumping invalid to a safe off-the-road stop.

The next half hour was bleak beyond description, a chapter in my life that I care to forget. The shouting, complaining, whining, crying and whimpering that came from that man during the tire changing in that ninety-six-degree day on that hot southern Illinois highway was enough to make me wish I'd entered the convent twenty years earlier.

During the next two hours of tears, intermingled with impregnable silence, I made my decision. Two days of continuing like this was more than this human body could bear, so in my calmest voice I explained how nice the trip would be for everyone if I simply took the two-year-old and made the rest of the trip by air. That way there would be plenty of room for the three older kids and Genghis Kahn.

When I explained how I'd saved the money for the airfare by couponing vigorously the previous year, the driver nodded in agreement and drove Wee One and myself to the nearest airport.

By the time the rest of the entourage arrived at our Gulf-side vacation home, I'd already taught the two-year-old how to swim, was a master at Irene's new microwave oven and had a great start on a nice tan.

We all shared stories about our trips down and finished off the vacation amidst mosquitoes, merriment and mayhem. The trip home was rather uneventful. The Vacation Wizard and his three stooges blew bubbles, sang loudly and snacked their way back into Yankee territory.

Me? I read three magazines, watched a movie, dined on macadamia nuts and a club sandwich, and sipped a lovely beverage. The flight attendants took turns entertaining the two-year-old and the whole thing went off without a hitch.

We're already planning next year's vacation. We're driving to Disneyland. I'm thinking about a part-time job in the meantime. Airfares will probably be higher by then.

Life's Too Short to Cry over Lost Power

WORLD WAR II WAS OVER, the 1940s had ended with a bang, and Dad was building his dream house, a three-bedroom ranch on three lots.

"Ed," my Grandma Knapp would say, "with all that electricity in the house, what will you ever do if the power goes off?"

"Oh, Maude," he'd answer, slightly exasperated at his old-fashioned mother-in-law, "all the new homes these days are dependent upon electricity. It's better than a natural resource. You never run out of electricity!"

"Suppose the power goes off in a storm? Lightning can knock out electric power," Grandma persisted.

"When that happens, it's just for a few minutes, then the power goes right back on. This is the twentieth century, Maude. Folks all over the country are heating and cooking with electricity, lighting their homes and running all sorts of handy appliances with it. There's nothing to worry about."

"Well, I'm just glad that you're building a fireplace in that house of yours," Grandma huffed. "At least you'll have heat when the power does go off."

Pop and Maude, my mother's father and stepmother,

lived three hours south of our home in Rock Falls, Illinois, in an old frame house on the outskirts of Blandinsville, population six hundred. They still heated their house with a coal stove in the living room, cooked their food and heated their bathwater on a woodstove in the kitchen, and made use of the outhouse out back. They had electrical wiring for lights but that was all. Grandpa and Grandma Knapp were living in a time warp.

When my dad started building our new home with radiant heat powered by an electric circulating pump (hot water pipes under the concrete floor that kept all the floors toasty warm in the winter), and when he built an indoor bathroom with a toilet that flushed with the aid of an electric motor on the pressure pump, and when he went out and purchased an electric stove, my grandparents shook their heads reprimandingly. In their minds, electricity was unreliable, unproven and confusing as all get out.

The next Christmas, Grandpa and Grandma were visiting for the holidays. So were my aunt and uncle and their three children from Alabama, who had driven up to our northern home during the holidays to enjoy the snowy cold *white* Christmas week.

That year, besides plenty of white, we got an ice storm to boot. It was just a day or two after Christmas when we awoke to a breathtaking sight. Ice hung heavy on the trees in glorious snowflake patterns.

We also woke up to the sound of silence. No radio. No boiler sound in the utility room spewing out hot water to heat the house. Not even the hum of the electric clock in the living room. Just silence. The power was off. It seems the beautiful ice had also weighed down the power lines so heavily that a few of the main trunk lines had snapped.

Dad reassured his house full of company, "It's just temporary. Power's never off for more than a few minutes, an hour at the most. Meanwhile, I'll just light a fire in the fireplace."

Grandma smiled and pulled a shawl up over her shoulders.

An hour turned into a day and Dad found himself walking two blocks down the road to a neighbor's house, a neighbor who still had a well and a hand pump out in front of his house. Dad filled two buckets and walked back to our house, slopping water as he walked in the snow. He gave one bucket of water to my mother for cooking and washing dishes, and poured the other into the toilet so it could be flushed. Every few hours he repeated the trek for two more buckets.

That night my mom, dad, brother, sister, aunt, uncle, three cousins, grandparents and I all brought blankets and quilts out to the living room and huddled around the fireplace. It was a grand slumber party, although I'm not sure how much sleep the adults got on that concrete floor in which the hot water pipes, now cold, were encased.

The next morning we awoke to the sound of silence again. Still no power. Grandma sat in her rocking chair, smiling with a twinkle in her eye, and told us kids stories about the good old days.

Meanwhile, Dad rigged up some sort of cooking rack

so Mom and my aunt could at least warm up vegetables and meats in the fireplace. That evening we popped popcorn over the open fire in a special screen popper. And even though it had a burned taste, my cousins and I loved the adventure of watching it pop over the open fire.

Later that evening Dad brought in a few old kerosene lamps he'd kept as collectors' items. At least we could recognize each other and not kick over the water buckets after dark.

By the third day, the whole romantic notion of roughing it inside the house was starting to wear thin. Dad was getting tired of hauling water from the neighbor's house and flushing the toilet for a dozen people. Mom was running out of fireplace food ideas. And no matter how much wood was burned in the fireplace, that large ranch home was still cold in every room except the living room.

Grandma kept the old cane rocker warm, sitting there rocking and smiling. I think she liked being from the turn-of-the-century generation. But more than that, I think she enjoyed the fact that those newfangled electric homes weren't all they were cut out to be after all. She never did say, "I told you so," but we all knew she was thinking it.

The power outage lasted four days, close to ninety-six hours. Practically an eternity for an electricity-dependent family like ours.

It lasted long enough for Dad to purchase an old-fashioned pitcher-spout hand pump that he could attach to the well (after disconnecting the electric pump) in the event the power ever went out again. At least he'd never have to haul water in buckets from the neighbors.

Even though I was a small girl during those four days after Christmas when the power went off, I still remember the simple pleasures of those quiet evenings. Huddled in blankets we read, sang, played cards by kerosene lamp, told stories, roasted marshmallows in the fireplace and talked about what needed to be done to get ready for the next time the power went off.

It never did, but it sure was fun planning for it. And at my home today, we have a wood burner with a cookstove top, a full cord of wood and a hand pump, just in case.

Life's Too Short for Sentimental Cards

I LIKE CONTEMPORARY, funny greeting cards for every occasion. Well, maybe not for people who have lost a loved one, but for all other occasions I search out the funniest, most hilarious greeting cards I can find. I gave my son Michael, the assistant director of the University of Wisconsin marching band, a card that said, "My trained dog Otto, here, is going to play a piece of classical music for your birthday, but don't worry . . . his Bach is worse than his bite!" For my little brother, nine years my junior, "Happy Birthday! Here's hoping you celebrate with your usual class and style . . . and this time, try not to get your head caught in the toilet seat!" Even for weddings I think a funny card reminds a couple that a sense of humor is probably the most important ingredient to a happy marriage.

In my home office I have a contemporary greeting card taped to the wall over my computer. It's a wild howling dog in a prize-fighter pose with arms straight up in the air and mouth open wide enough to hold a football. In bright red, yellow and blue letters it proclaims, KICK SOME BUTT! KICK SOME BUTT! KICK SOME BUTT! Inside it says simply, "There, consider yourself encouraged." That card makes me laugh and inspires me to work hard, do my best and grab for all the gusto in life as I set out each morning to eke out a career in my home office.

One time years ago, when I was still married, I remember giving my husband a card for Valentine's Day with a photograph of two bananas on the front. Inside, the card simply said, "You're driving me bananas, but I love you anyway."

He gave me one of those gloppy, flower-filled, serious cards. I honestly didn't even bother to read all the words because it was a long rhyming poem that was even gloppier than the hearts and flowers all over the front.

On our second anniversary he sent me his typical mushy card. "Together as we look ahead and future years unfold, may we know all the happiness two loving hearts can hold." He signed it with lots of X's and O's. My card to him for that same anniversary was homemade. The drawing wasn't too spectacular, but the words were true to my slapstick style. "He loves his life, treasures his wife, works very hard, takes care of the yard, speaks in verse, is always terse . . . oh dear, somebody slap me." At least my feelings of love, dipped in humor, were original and not written by some nerdy guy at Hallmark who probably speaks in rhyme all the time.

Anyway, for the first few years of our marriage, I continued to howl at the funny, pun-filled, silly cards I sent my husband. And Harold continued to say, "Did you read the words?" after I opened his cards, quickly glanced at the signature at the bottom and then said, "Thank you." (He knew I hadn't read the long rhyming poem.)

Then one year I was thanking my mother for some beautiful cloth dinner napkins she'd given me for my birthday. "What a perfect gift, Mom! How did you know I wanted napkins?"

"Simple," she said. "You've been giving cloth napkins to everyone lately—for shower gifts, birthday gifts, wedding gifts. People often give what they themselves want."

She was right. I did give what I really wanted. I thought about the greeting cards I bought for people. I realized I not only wanted to give funny, contemporary cards, I wanted to receive them, too.

Then I thought about my husband. He obviously liked those sentimental greeting cards because he had a need to read those soft, romantic words. Perhaps he needed to be reassured of my love in a more serious way than I did. He was giving what he, himself, wanted to receive.

After that, whenever I bought greeting cards for Harold, I looked for special, meaningful, serious declarations of my love. In spite of the fact that those mushy poems made me feel as if I was adding a quart of honey to a quart of sugar and maple syrup and then spreading it on a slathering of strawberry jam over toast, I gave him what he wanted and needed—rhyming verse that oozed with sentimentality.

Perhaps we all need to look more carefully into the hearts and personalities of our loved ones when buying gifts and greeting cards. I know I, for one, had to learn to give with the receiver's needs in mind, not what I found appealing. I had to learn that to "kick some butt" in the gift-giving department might mean buying pink puppy dogs on a bed of hearts, flowers and lace. (Oh, gag me.) But at least now I smile, wrap it up and give it gladly.

Life's Too Short to Fly Alone

ONE OF MY FAVORITE TOPICS of conversation with my dad is about his days as a World War II fighter pilot. I recall many stories of his flights over the Pacific Ocean where he, as flight leader of four planes, led his wing man, the second element leader and that man's wing man (also known as "Tail End Charlie") out over the big drink of the South Pacific into combat with the Japanese.

The four P-39s, flying in perfect synchronization, would stay together in a semi-V formation. If enemy planes were spotted, the flight leader would issue the order to his wing man, second element leader and Tail End Charlie to crisscross back and forth in a wide scissors pattern, doing giant figure eights in the sky. The advantage, of course, of flying in groups of four in such a complicated maneuver, rather than going it alone, was protection. Their four-plane flight formation allowed two planes to protect and cover the other two if the enemy attacked from either side.

The idea of in-flight teamwork was reinforced for me not long ago when I read an explanation about why geese always fly in a V formation:

As each bird flaps its wings, it creates an uplift for the bird immediately following. By flying in V formation, the whole flock adds at least seventy-one percent greater flying range than if each bird flew on its own.

When a goose falls out of formation, it suddenly feels the drag and resistance of trying to go it alone—and quickly gets back into formation to take advantage of the lifting power of the bird in front.

When the head goose gets tired, it rotates back in the wing and another goose flies point. Geese honk from behind to encourage those up front to keep up their speed.

Finally, when a goose gets sick or is wounded by gunshot, and falls out of formation, two other geese fall out with that goose and follow it down to lend help and protection. They stay with the fallen goose until it is able to fly or until it dies; and only then do they launch out on their own or with another formation to catch up with their group. (Author unknown)

Seems to me we could all use a few lessons from fighter pilots and geese when it comes to using teamwork to solve many of life's problems, especially the ones encountered along the way during our parenting journeys.

As parents we flap our wings, trying to teach our children how to walk, talk, learn, obey rules and be polite. We encourage our children to follow our behavior, so they can become stronger and fly higher and higher. But sometimes it's hard for the little ones to keep up. They get tired or cranky. That's when we have to slow down, stop, soothe their feelings and offer encouragement, just as the geese do when one of their flock falls out of formation. Usually our children respond to our soft touch, gentle voice and motivating words, and before we know it, they're right back on track, flying high. Sometimes they squawk and pitch a fit. But we stay with them and continue to offer encouragement until they're ready to join the rest of the family.

Once in a while Mom and Dad get tired of leading and, like the head goose, they want a break. So they go to the back of the line and let the rest of the family lead the entourage toward their goal for a while. When a parent needs a rest from the stress of flying point bird, it's important that the other members step in immediately to offer encouragement and moral support . . . . just as the geese do when they honk from behind to encourage those up front to keep up their speed. Amazing, isn't it, how just a little encouragement from other members of the flock can help us fly straight, fast and free?

Finally, when Mom, Dad, Grandpa or Grandma get sick or wounded (even if it's a temporary spiritual, physical or mental wounding), one or more of us needs to fall out of formation completely and go to their aid. It may be inconvenient, cause us to lose work time or play time, but that's what families do. They, like the geese, care for the sick or wounded for as long as it takes, until they have recovered or died.

It is only then, when we have acted selflessly to help the others in our flock, that we can truly say we are a creature of God, as courageous as a fighter pilot and as noble as the geese flying in the uplifting V formation.

Chapter Five

Lifestyles of the Poor and Not-So-Famous

Don't you love how real life keeps you humble? Anyone who was not born being fed by a nanny using sterling silver spoons and dinging little silver bells to summon the butler who then calls up the Rolls Royce driver to fetch the pabulum knows that real life isn't like that.

Most of us were born in simple families with hardworking parents and were taught values that somehow propel us through a lifetime of major and minor struggles. And since struggles are those things that ultimately make us strong, give us good character and help us become much more interesting people, we ordinary folk learn to love our struggles. We cherish them! And would we honestly want to change our lives to be suddenly rich and famous? The answer for me, at least, a single parent of four children and seven grandchildren, who is no doubt at the midpoint in her life (I'm hoping to live to be at least 110), is that I can honestly say that I am too happy in my simple life to even consider being rich and famous. I mean it. Yes, I do. I really, really mean it.

Life's Too Short
to Wear Brand Names

THERE SHE GOES, out the door toward the school bus in her Jordache jeans, Izod alligator shirt, Adidas shoes and her London Fog jacket. There she goes . . . the neighbor's kid, not mine.

My daughters, unfortunately, were just as label-conscious, but fortunately I'm not. I remember those years when they were teenagers, running for the bus in their RS jeans. Never heard of that brand? RS stands for "rummage sale," a buck fifty at a dandy five-family sale down the block.

Their shirts were genuine HMDs (hand-me-downs) given to us graciously by my younger sister, who has great taste in clothes and never wore anything out.

Their shoes? A fine label, loved by mothers everywhere: TRAX. "Attention K-Mart shoppers, today's blue light special is located in the shoe department where our TRAX shoes are . . ."

We never did go the Levis, Anne Klein, Nike route when my kids were growing up. Instead we went to this sale, that sale, everywhere a sale-sale. And instead of being walking billboards for rich clothing manufacturers, my children emerged with a sense of well-defined individuality, wearing fashions that they liked and were comfortable in, even if they were already broken in a little.

That snappy zippered jacket was an honest-to-goodness "Seven Miler." Two bucks at the Seven-Mile Fair, the biggest flea market north of the Illinois-Wisconsin border. It's a great place to shop for school clothes, hubcaps, chickens, fresh vegetables, pet rabbits, spray paint, old dishes and screwdriver sets. Once I even found a genuine pair of used Gloria Vanderbilt jeans there. Of course, I ripped the label off before I took them home to my daughter. I figured once she squeezed her little backside into a pair of designer label jeans, there'd be no going back to no-name land.

I have to admit, the label battle lasted at my house off and on for years, until my second daughter was out of college, completely on her own, paying her own bills, buying her own clothes. Now that she's a mother of three, I love watching her take great pride in buying most of her kids' clothes at rummage sales.

When my children go shopping in today's label-crazed world, I hope they will recall their growing up years and realize that there are more important things to do with your money than pad the pockets of the owners of overpriced designer fashions. I hope that now that they're grown and buying clothes for their own kids, they'll retain the same sense of prudent frugality that I, by necessity, taught them as children.

Life's Too Short
to keep Changing My Name

NICKNAMES, SURNAMES, maiden names, married names, stage names, pen names, birth names. Why do we keep changing our names?

Why is it that most women take their husband's surname as their own when they marry? They end up spending the rest of their lives referring to their *real* names as their *maiden* names. Think about it. *Maiden name* is the name of an unmarried woman, one who has not yet married and acquired her husband's name. It's as if she's in a state of limbo before marriage . . . just waiting for that grand day when she gets her official name, i.e., her husband's. I say, "Phooey!"

Even those women who do keep their maiden names after marriage must go through life explaining, "Yes, I'm married, but I decided to keep my maiden name."

A person's name is an important birthright, a definite statement of who that person is. Our *real* birth name is as individual as our personality, intelligence and physical traits. Whether we succeed or fail in life, shouldn't the same name—first, middle and last—accompany each of us from birth to death?

Men, for the most part, exercise their undeniable right

to their name . . . the same name from birth certificate to tombstone. Why can't women do the same?

A name, given at birth, tells the world who we are. Why should we confuse our friends, relatives, neighbors, employers, businesses, government agencies and fans by periodically changing the one thing that separates us from the rest of humanity?

I don't have the answers to these questions. I, for one, am guilty of this name-changing silliness. I have changed my name, or parts of it, seven times. I'm ashamed of myself. As a matter of fact, I'm beginning to wonder, *Who am I and why do I keep changing my name?*

It all started simply. Patricia Ann Kobbeman. That's what my parents wrote on my birth certificate. A nice, simple Scottish-Irish-English-French-German-and-Dutch name.

If you said it right, it even rhymed. Ann with man. Oh sure, there were the usual nicknames: P.K., Patsy Ann, Pattyricia. A few goofballs in high school insisted on Kobby. But basically, it was a good name.

It even looked symmetrical, with eight letters in the first and last names and the neat three-letter Ann tucked in the middle. That rhyming, symmetrical beauty held up for twenty-two years. Then, in a moment of prefeminist flutter, I gave it up to take my husband's last name when I married. I became Patricia Ann Taylor.

Seven years later, when the marriage failed, I tried to ease the pain with levity . . . telling friends the only reason I'd married him in the first place was so my initials would spell my first name, P.A.T.

I moved out of state and grabbed a job at a radio station in northern Illinois. My duties included doing a live show each morning called *What's Going On*. My show provided free publicity for any club, church, school, organization or nonprofit group in a four-county area.

I'd blabber on about how much fun a person could have at the oyster-chili supper at the United Methodist Church, or at the all-you-can-eat pancake and fish fest at the Rod and Gun Club. My name, Pat Taylor, became synonymous with free publicity and therefore hung on the lips of every organizer of every event in the dozen towns within earshot of the radio station.

Three years later, I remarried and changed identities once again. When I took my second husband's name I became Pat Lorenz. My radio boss, however, not wanting to confuse the listeners, insisted that the queen of free publicity keep the name Pat Taylor.

What new bride wants to continue using her first husband's name? I compromised by tacking on my new name at the end. Now, I was Pat Taylor-Lorenz. That aberration lasted about two weeks.

The main problem with that name was that the two "lors" right in the middle made it a tongue tangler. And radio folks, especially, don't take a great liking to tongue-twister names for their on-air staff. So it wasn't long before the radio people shortened my name to Pat Tay-lorenz.

I hated that mutation. The Tay part was like a brick around my neck, constantly reminding me of my first husband and his abusive drinking, which led to the end of the marriage. Six months later, when I became pregnant and quite gutsy, not only from the side view, but emotionally, I had a heart-to-heart talk with my radio listeners. "So from now on, folks," I concluded, "my name is simply Pat Lorenz." Somehow, the boss let me get away with it.

The next year I moved to Wisconsin and started a career as a freelance writer. I thought about taking a pen name, like Penworthy Waddington or Rebecca Farmer, but I just couldn't face another name change. I decided to keep it simple. My friends and family knew me as Pat Lorenz, so that's what my byline would be.

A few months later it dawned on me that the name Pat could be mistaken for a man's name. Some writer friends said they believed men get more attention from editors than women. I was enough of a feminist to know that in good conscience I didn't want to win editorial favor because some editor might think I was a man. No sir. If I was going to be a successful writer, by golly, I was going to do it without a doubt as to whether Pat was a man or a woman. So I changed my name again, or at least formalized and feminized it to Patricia A. Lorenz, my legal, check-signing signature.

For two years my manuscripts were printed with that byline. My husband, figuring I'd finally found a name I liked and planned to use the rest of my life, started buying me gifts with that name imprinted on everything. Patricia A. Lorenz headlined a five-year supply of stationery, fifty dozen manila envelope labels, a box of one thousand business cards, an imprint gizmo that only an idiot would take time to use and a desk sign with my name forged in brazen two-inch-high letters. Since my office is tucked in the furthest corner downstairs in my home and I'm the only person who ever sees the desk, he must have thought the pressure of being a freelance writer would someday make me forget who I am and that I'd need that name sign to remind me. How did he know it would happen just like that?

In spite of all the name-labeled supplies, the more I thought about my name, the more I hated that formal-looking-and-sounding A jammed in the middle. If I was going to be a famous, prolific writer, I should have a name that rolls off one's lips in lilting syllables, like Barbara Walters, Sophia Loren, Annette Funicello.

After all, how many famous people actually use those middle initials in everyday life? I thought to myself. I could only think of two. Ulysses S. Grant and John F. Kennedy. So I dropped the A.

Not long after that, my second marriage ended with a whimper, and two years after the divorce my second husband, the man who'd given me my third surname, passed on to his final reward. Now I don't have a living relative whose name is Lorenz. Except for my four children, of course, three of whom changed their last names from Taylor to Lorenz when I married my second husband.

Not long ago my eldest daughter, feminist and artist Jeanne Lorenz, declared that she's never going to change her name. "That's the spirit!" I told her joyfully. "The same moniker from birth certificate to death certificate!"

Then I remembered: Her birth certificate says Jeanne Marie Taylor.

Oh dear, who are we anyway, and why do we keep changing our names?

Life's Too Short to Let the Cold Get you Down

AFTER TWENTY YEARS of driving buses for the county transit system, John Williams thought he'd seen everything. But something happened one cold December day in Milwaukee that changed all that.

John was worrying about his problems just like the next guy. Wondering how he was going to pay the December gas bill. Wondering if he'd be able to buy any Christmas presents that year. Wondering if he was ever going to get ahead of the game.

On that cold, dreary, gray-sky day just before Christmas, the temperature was ten degrees and it was trying to snow. Every time John opened the bus door a blast of cold air slapped him in the face.

"Lousy time of year," John grumbled, "just plain lousy."

As usual, around 3:00 PM, John was driving his bus down Wisconsin Avenue. At Marquette High School he picked up the usual group of students. It seemed to John that as Christmas drew closer, the high-school boys grew louder and more rowdy. Pushing and shoving, they stumbled to the back of the bus.

Rich kids, John mumbled to himself disgustedly. Most of the boys from the prep school lived in the ritzier suburbs and would be transferring off his bus in a mile or so.

A few stops later, John pulled up in front of the Milwaukee County Medical Complex grounds where a woman was waiting in the bus shelter. She looked about forty years old, pregnant, and her dingy gray coat was tattered from collar to hem. When she pulled herself up the steps of the bus, John noticed she was only wearing socks, no shoes.

"Good Lord, woman, where are your shoes?" he blurted out without thinking. "It's too cold to be out without shoes! Get on in here and off that cold sidewalk!"

The woman struggled up the steps, pulling her gray buttonless coat around her protruding belly. "Never mind my shoes. This bus goin' downtown?"

Still staring at her feet John answered, "Well, eventually we'll get back downtown. Have to head west first, then we'll turn around."

"I don't mind the extra ride, long as I can get warm. Lordy, it's cold out there. Wind must be comin' off the lake!" she sighed as she handed John her money and sat down on the front seat.

The high-school kids in the back started in. "Hey, lady, nice coat! That a Saks Fifth Avenue special? Doesn't she know we don't serve patrons without shoes?"

John felt like strangling every one of those kids. To distract the woman from their remarks, he continued his conversation, "Yup, it's a rough time of year all right."

The woman sat up straight in her seat and smoothed the wrinkles in her coat. "Sure is. I got eight kids. Had enough money this year to buy shoes for every one of 'em, but that was it. I got some slippers at home, but I didn't want to get 'em all wet in case it snowed."

John kept the conversation going. "Yup. It ain't easy with Christmas and all. Money's scarce. And if this weather doesn't warm up, I'm wonderin' if I'll have enough to pay the gas bill."

"Mister, you just be glad you got a place to live and a job. The good Lord will take care of you. Always has for me."

John couldn't believe that a woman who didn't have on any shoes was telling *him* to stop worrying.

Before long the bus was at the end of the line, time for the kids to get off and transfer to other buses that would take them to their comfortable suburban homes.

As the boys filed off, one young student named Frank, a fourteen-year-old freshman who had been sitting just a few seats behind the woman in the gray tattered coat, stopped in front of her and handed her his new leather sport shoes. "Here, lady, you take these. You need 'em more than I do."

And with that, Frank walked off the bus and into the ten-degree evening in his stocking feet.

When the woman tried on the shoes she let out a whoop and a holler, "Why, they fit perfect! Can you believe that? Perfect. Nice and warm, too. Bless the Lord. Mister, I told you not to worry 'bout nothin'. Don't you see? The Lord always provides. Always." Somehow, for

John Williams, that busy Christmas season was better than all the other years put together.

John says his faith in God and in humankind was completely restored on that cold, gray day in Milwaukee on a bus heading west by a woman wearing a very expensive pair of sport shoes.

Life's Too Short to Get Sick

THERE'S SOMETHING ABOUT being sick and being a parent that doesn't mesh. The very instant we give birth, it seems that all mothers are slapped on the back with a bright red bumper sticker: CAREGIVER. NO SICK DAYS ALLOWED.

Mothers understand what I'm talking about. It's the rule, the unspoken, unwritten, but very-much-in-existence rule about how long a mother is allowed to be sick. I think the rule says something like two or three hours every fifth, even-numbered year in a month that ends in *E*.

Don't get me wrong, I'm not a bellyaching sort of person who conjures up imagined headaches or three-day flu bouts, the way some people do, just to get a break from the routine. I just think mothers deserve a little more consideration than most families seem willing to give when she is sick. And that's why I'm spouting off.

I remember the last time I had the flu as if it were the day before yesterday. The year was 1987. I left work early that day, head pounding, body shivering, glands aching, nose sniveling, mouth dry, chest full.

The drive home was no basket of cherries either, in all that snow. As I tried to keep the car on the road I wondered, *Why couldn't I get sick in July and lie on the cool sheets in my underwear and sip cold drinks until the fever passed?*

At home, that cold, gray, December day, I undressed, pulled on my bleakest-looking, washed out, dark blue jogging suit with the elastic waist and ankles, popped two extra-strength cold tablets, slid between the flannel sheets, and pulled three blankets, a bedspread and a heating pad over my body.

It was 2:20 PM. I could sleep for an hour before my oldest daughter arrived home from high school. I'd already made arrangements for a neighbor to take her to her piano lesson at 4:00 PM.

At 3:40 PM the two junior high teens would be waltzing in the door, stomachs growling, ready to eat Milwaukee. One of them would walk to the babysitter's to pick up the five-year-old. If I got out of bed now and wrote them a note telling them I was sick and to please be quiet and let me sleep, I might even make it a two-hour nap.

So I wrote the note. Back in bed I dreamt of the day when the children would all be grown and I wouldn't have to write them any more notes. Just letters telling them I'd be jetting out to Denver, Phoenix, New York City or wherever they all lived by then. I'd tell them to get the guest room ready and that I'd take them out to dinner in a fancy restaurant. After a long, luxurious candlelit meal, we'd walk to one of those elegant round restaurants that rotates ever so slowly on top of a skyscraper and order an oversize fruit drink with a name that sounds like a Hawaiian volcano, and we'd talk about our exciting, fulfilling lives. Later, I'd fall asleep in the guest room of their new condominium. . . .

Aaaaa-choooo! The phone rang. "Hi, Mom. I hate to tell you this, but you know I have my drum lesson after school and I forgot my drumsticks and music. Could you bring 'em down right away?"

The front door opened. "Mom! Where are you? I brought Lisa home with me so we could practice our new cheers in the family room with that new cheerleading record". . . a sentence hollered for the benefit of the neighbors down the street, instead of for poor little ol' me, sniveling and shivering in my bedroom.

I thought to myself, *I deserve this bed, this rest, this heating pad. I deserve some quiet time. I've earned it. No matter what they say, holler, do, demand or plead, I'm just going to lie here and be sick. Of course, I'll feel a little glum because they haven't learned the art of proper "mother pampering," but in the meantime I'll try my darndest to get well. After all, even if it is written in the book on what being a mother is all about—that we aren't supposed to get sick (at least not take-to-the-bed kind of sick)—I can't help this. I ache all over. My toes ache. My hair aches. I need quiet. My teenagers will just have to survive without me.*

Aaaaa-choooo!

By 9:00 AM of day two (after somehow getting them all off to school amidst one exaggerated crisis after another), I practically overdosed on flu and cold medicine, trying desperately to get my shambles-of-a-household back in order. By evening of day two the whole family was mad at me for being sick. I had to beg the oldest to come and sit in my room and talk to me. I was lonely, but did they care?

I paged through my Bible. There it was, proof that mothers weren't supposed to get sick. Right there in Matthew 8:14 (TLB): "When Jesus arrived at Peter's house, Peter's mother-in-law was in bed with a high fever. But when Jesus touched her hand, the fever left her; and she got up and prepared a meal for them!"

I'm sorry to say that by ten o'clock that night I actually wondered where Jesus was when I needed Him.

By morning of day three I figured that I would feel just as bad whether I was lying on the living room sofa or in my bed. The sofa at least provided a centrally located place from which to direct family life and/or at least help solve one crisis after another.

By day four I couldn't take it anymore and was off to work, still sneezing and aching but having learned my lesson that it's impossible for a mother, especially a single parent, to escape under the covers for four days without the entire household threatening mutiny.

I learned my lesson that year. Getting sick is simply not in the mother's handbook of life. Since then I've only thrown up once. I resumed my phone conversation two minutes later and went to work twenty minutes after that. I figure that by the time my youngest has graduated from college, then, and only then, can I legally afford to get sick. In the meantime I feel a shiver coming on, but we mothers know that means it's simply time to pull on the long underwear and forge ahead with gusto.

Life's Too Short to Keep Stuff

IS IT ME OR DOES IT HAPPEN to everyone after age fifty? I'm referring to the need to get rid of things; to clean out the clutter in the house, garage, attic, shed and office; to stop shopping once and for all; to stop looking for more drop-dead bargains at every rummage sale I see on a Saturday morning; to eat everything in the cupboards, refrigerator and freezer before I buy another thing; and finally, to have rummage sales where everything is free, so people who can truly use my excess clutter and junk can have it without worrying about price and I won't have to lug it all to Goodwill or Human Concerns.

I don't think it's just me. I think middle age causes most of us finally to get hold of ourselves and realize that the constant need to build, change and improve the nest dwindles and finally disappears altogether around the half-century mark.

Recently the "Get rid of stuff!" mood hit me. I filled my large dining room table with old housewares, jewelry and books to give away to all the women who showed up at my monthly "interesting women" group. I had one rule that night. They couldn't leave until they found something on the table to take home with them. They grumbled, but they obeyed. That's what happens when you have hosted a women's group for every gathering since 1989. The women are so glad they don't have to have to host it, they'll do almost anything to humor you.

As I was going through one of my numerous shelves for books to give away, I came across one of those blank "Write Your Own Book" books. I'd given it to my mother on May 14, 1978, just two months after she'd learned, at age fifty-six, that she had a terminal illness. Inside the cover I wrote, "Dear Mom, I'm giving you this book for you to fill with all the love that's inside you, so that someday you can give it back and I'll treasure it for all time. Thank you for being the most wonderful mother imaginable and for being such a good friend. I love you. Happy Mother's Day. Love, Pat."

In her neat, small, beautiful handwriting, Mother made only six entries in that book. Her illness, Lou Gehrig's disease, quickly took away her ability to write. Her last entry was dated November 8, 1978. She died the following year on August 1.

As I paged through the empty pages of my mother's "Write Your Own Book" that day, a scrap of paper fell out. In shaky handwriting that was not so neat, my mother had written the following words:

> We squander health in search of wealth;
> We scheme and toil and save.
> Then squander wealth in search of health
> And all we get is a grave.
> We live and boast of what we own,
> Then die and only get a stone.

I'm not sure if they're my mother's words or if she copied them from somebody else, but as her health declined I watched her search her soul, her mind and her past experiences to find the meaning of life. That little poem must have captured how she felt about the eventual uselessness of *things*.

Like most of us, my mother spent a great deal of her life building her nest. She was a lover and collector of antiques, a hobby that I have inherited. My dad built the home I grew up in, and together they furnished it lovingly and beautifully with antiques and bits of this and that found at estate sales and auctions. Thanks to my dad's ability to repair and refinish the oldest of the old, their house and barn gradually filled up with one treasure after another to become a showpiece of decorating finesse.

But there she was, at age fifty-six, writing one of the last things she would ever write, scribbled in her shaky handwriting, a poem about the futility of possessions. I wondered if Mom would have done things differently if she'd had her life to live over.

So many of us spend our whole lives acquiring things. We work so hard to buy the house, furniture, housewares, cars, campers, vans, bikes, boats, TVs, toys, music systems, computers, games, gadgets and gizmos that in the process we forget that all we're going to have at the end is a gravestone.

A month before I turned fifty, I made a promise to myself to stop shopping. I promised that I would give away at least three boxes of things to my friends and family each year. I also made a solemn promise to myself that I wouldn't buy any clothes for three years.

These days my house is much neater and far less cluttered. And I'm finally wearing out all three closets full of clothes that I have accumulated over the previous fifteen years. I doubt if I'll ever like shopping again. Believe me, the sense of freedom when you stop shopping is exhilarating! I leave you with my poem.

It's about morning walks and lengthy talks.
Smelling flowers, enjoying showers.
For writing books, exploring nooks.
I'll squander not my health for wealth.
For when I die, I'll call your bluff.
I'll leave my thoughts, instead of stuff.

Life's Too Short to Miss a Road Trip with your Brother

I VISITED MY SON ANDREW in Tempe at the Arizona State University campus one May when the temperature was 106 degrees, and in order to get anywhere we had to wait in the sun for the city buses. I quickly understood why he needed a car, so I flew home to Wisconsin and purchased a 1986 old beater from a pilot friend. "Runs good. Just has a little rust is all, and there's no air-conditioning," he said when I wrote out the check.

After talking my brother Joe into joining me on the trip to deliver the car, I warned him that there was no air-conditioning in the gray beast. "That's okay," he joked, "I'll just drive naked."

We dubbed the up-and-coming trip "The First Annual Naked Road Trip across America." We didn't follow through, of course, considering the viewpoint of those truck drivers in their eighteen-wheelers, but we sure wanted to take it all off a number of times during our long, hot trip.

I have to say the car ran like a champ during the entire journey. It was just the unbelievable heat that got us. I met Joe on Sunday afternoon in Des Moines, Iowa, where he flew in from Louisville, Kentucky. Since I'd already been on the road driving from my home in Milwaukee for nearly eight hours and he was fresh as a spring daisy, he drove the gray beast until 11:30 that night when we arrived, like two zombies, in Wichita, Kansas.

The next day, Joe and I personally experienced purgatory, hell and the wrath of the fire dragon. Kansas, Oklahoma, Texas and New Mexico were so hot that day and the car so much like the inside of a massive restaurant-sized oven that we poured water and ice down our underwear.

To take our minds off the heat we decided to punctuate our adventure with amazing wonders of the world. Having decided to take the back roads instead of the interstate, we came upon some "Let's get out of this infernal car!" sights, including the world's largest hand-dug well . . . thirty-two feet in diameter by 109 feet deep, into which we climbed with glee. There's nothing more refreshing than being 109 feet down in a well when you just got out of the ovenlike car.

Next we saw two feed lots in Texas with more grazing beef cattle than you could possibly imagine, nigh on a quarter-million, we estimated. It stretched for miles and those cows were packed in so tight that at first I couldn't even see them—I thought it was all landscape. Joe pulled onto a gravel side road, so I could get up close and personal. We climbed a fence, held up our big bag of beef jerky in front of them and took a picture, which is captioned, "Oh dear, see what you fellas have to look forward to?"

After another few hours of the driving inferno, we visited the VLA in New Mexico, which stands for "Very Large Array," the world's largest radio telescope. Each of the twenty-seven dish-shaped antennas weighs more than a 747 jumbo jet and they're all positioned on three tracks, each thirteen miles long, forming a Y. Each antenna collects incoming radio signals from distant galaxies. I didn't even know the folks in distant galaxies had radios.

From there the trip was filled with lots of brother-sister jawing on topics ranging from our kids and various practical jokes we could pull on them . . . to what we're going to do if our dad ever decides to slow down. We decided he probably never would, so it was a short conversation.

At the end of the third day, after stuffing ourselves with beef jerky, dry roasted nuts and red licorice for the past nine meals, we also talked a lot about how constipated we were and decided to do something about it. We stopped at a grocery, bought forty-eight ounces of prune juice, poured twenty-ounces each over ice and had us a prune cocktail right there in the parking lot. Needless to say, four hours later, when the juice did its magic in a big way, we both regretted that drink more than anything we have ever consumed in our lives.

But all in all, the trip across America was an adventure that taught me a number of things. First, all we really need in life are three things: water, food and sleep. It's possible to survive excessive heat and being very, very uncomfortable. Second, you can be happy, even in miserable circumstances, if you're with someone with a sense of humor. And third, it's easy to complain when you aren't comfortable, but it's a lot more pleasant, especially on a long, hot trip, to find the humor, adventure or even a few learning opportunities in the experience.

I, for one, learned that if you're lucky enough to have a brother, you need to take a car trip alone with him. Just go easy on the prune juice.

Chapter Six

Working World and Who Needs It

In 1992 I quit my regular job as a radio copywriter to stay home and write what I wanted to write. I'd written more than forty thousand radio commercials over the years, convincing people to buy stuff they didn't need or couldn't afford. I decided it was thirty-nine thousand too many commercials for one lifetime, so I quit.

It was the scariest thing I've ever done. I was a single parent with two kids in college, one in high school and one in grade school. What was I thinking? Nobody makes a living as a freelance writer with no boss and no regular assignments! But it was my dream, and I decided there were lots more important things I wanted from my life than a regular income and financial security.

Since that year, I've never earned as much money as I did in 1992, but I have never been happier. In fact, no matter what my income is, I get happier every single year. Why? Because I'm following my dream while I'm still awake. Nothing, no amount of stuff, can replace that feeling of doing what you love and using the talents God gave you.

Life's Too Short
to Worry about Anything

THE YEAR 1987 was Tom Trebelhorn's first year as manager of the Milwaukee Brewers baseball team. Two weeks
into the baseball season the Brewers made front page. The
headlines proclaimed, "Nieves Pitches Historic No-Hitter"
and "It's Brewer Time, Oh What a Night, Nieves, 9–0."

Nine and zero wasn't the score of the game. The Brewers
were undefeated. Nine wins and no losses at the start of the
season. Quite a feat, considering that just two weeks earlier
seasoned sportswriters in a national poll had predicted the
Brewers would come in seventh out of fourteen for the year
. . . if they were lucky. One sportswriter even wrote that the
Brewers' shortstop Dale Sveum "couldn't catch a cold if he
tried." Since the Brewers had ended the 1986 season in
twelfth place in the American League, those writers were
being generous.

But by mid-April the Brewers had struck gold. They
were the Cinderella team of the sports world, and Tom
Trebelhorn was their rookie manager. To top off the sweet
victory of their ninth straight win, Juan Nieves, one of the
Brewers' youngest players, starting his second year with
the club, had just pitched the first no-hitter in Brewers
baseball history, shutting out the Baltimore Orioles 7–0. No

doubt about it, the *True Blue Brew Crew* was loaded with magic. Brewers fans were hysterical. Fair-weather fans came out of the closet. The stands were packed.

Two days later, when the Brewers won their tenth in a row, the headlines shouted, *Treb's Triumph!* One radio station passed out plastic megaphones—"Trebelhorns," they called them. The media was helping to get the fans as hyped up as the team was.

The Brew Crew triumphed again on Saturday, April 18. The next morning, Easter Sunday, churchgoers and Easter-egg hunters in Milwaukee awoke to the headlines, *11th Heaven!!!!!*

Easter Sunday afternoon at Milwaukee County Stadium, under a Brewers-blue sky and a sunny seventy-five-degree day, the fans were feverish. Saturday's win had given the Brewers the league record for victories at the start of a season and had set a team record for consecutive wins in any season.

The thirty thousand fans, dressed in shorts, T-shirts, sunglasses and suntan lotion, looked like a bunch of laid-back surfer types. Some were wearing rabbit ears in the spirit of the holiday. The fans were so hyped up with Brewers fever that they gave howling standing ovations to pregame highlight films shown on the stadium's big screen. During the game they didn't even seem to mind that the first eight and a half innings were boring.

By the bottom of the ninth the hometown heroes were down 4–1. The Brewers were looking down the dark alley of their first loss of the year.

Glenn Braggs walked. Greg Brock singled. The crowd was on its feet. Some were actually pointing to the left field stands, where they believed Rob Deer would now deposit the pitch for a three-run homer to tie the game.

The ball slammed into left field. The fans went wild as the scoreboard proclaimed 4–4. Next, Jim Gantner walked. Now it was Dale Sveum's turn . . . the guy the sportswriters said "couldn't catch a cold if he tried." Those sportswriters hadn't said anything about Sveum's hitting ability. A few heads actually spun around that day when Sveum walked up to the plate and slammed a home run clear across the stadium to win the game 6–4. The crowd, already delirious from the tie, let out a deafening roar that lasted ten minutes. As the loudspeaker played songs like "I'm a Believer," those thirty thousand fans stomped, chanted, sung, hugged and danced for more than two hours after the game ended.

Never before had Brewers fever reached such a peak. In Chicago the next day against the White Sox, the Brewers didn't disappoint a single soul in Comiskey Park, except for a few die-hard Sox fans, that is. Brewers fans streamed into the stadium, after driving two hours in droves from Milwaukee to Chicago down Lake Michigan's shoreline.

There, in the heart of the "Windy City," the winning streak struck on, almost like a fairy tale. The score 13–0 meant the Milwaukee Brewers tied the record of wins-at-the-start-of-a-season by any team in baseball history, set by the Atlanta Braves in 1982. It was a sweet record, especially since the Braves used to be the *Milwaukee* Braves.

By now the Brewers had become an international sensation, the darlings of baseball around the world. Every minute with the team was a media event. The Brewers' games were even being broadcast worldwide by the Armed Forces radio network.

Then, without warning, the winning streak came to a screeching halt the next night when the White Sox stopped them cold in their tracks 7–1. The next week and a half the Brewers lost two more but won seven, bringing their record to twenty wins and three losses . . . and they were still the number one team in the country.

The following week the Brewers started another streak, a losing streak. After the seventh loss at home they captured another record, the worst home stand in Brewers history.

The tenth straight loss was a real ego-buster when they fell to the Kansas City Royals 13–0. By the time the team reached twelve straight losses, Brewers fever had turned ice-cold. The Brew Crew hung their heads. The national media had packed up and gone home. Local newspaper headlines scolded, *Brewers' Song Turns Gloomy* and *Brewers Can't Put Game Back Together Again.*

Tom Trebelhorn went from being the amazing rookie manager of the year at the helm of the number one baseball team in America to being the laughing stock of the sports world . . . all within six weeks. When asked how the team and coach were able to survive such fame followed up by jabs and ridicule, Treb answered, "You just don't worry about it."

When questioned further, Trebelhorn explained, "I used to worry . . . a lot. When I was coaching the minor leagues, I'd fuss and fume and stay at the park for hours after a game, wondering where I went wrong if we lost. I'd go over every play, trying to make it right in my mind. Then I'd set up every single detail for the next day's game, making sure the right person was scheduled to play in the right order to assure success. Often I didn't get home until one or two in the morning. It sure wasn't much of a life for my wife and children.

"And if one of those minor league teams would be losing game after game, I'd really work myself into a snit worrying about why we lost. When I'd finally make it home after a game I'd sulk quietly, refusing to share my pain with my wife and three young sons. I shut them out of my life and nurtured my worries instead.

"Well, I worried myself right into a divorce, which wasn't too surprising. After all, communication, the basis of every good marriage, hadn't found its way into our lives. For me, it was all baseball and worry.

"Years before, I worried when I couldn't get out of the minor leagues as a player. I wanted more than anything to get on a major league team. One time I got traded up to the Oakland A's, but I never got to play on the big team. Before long I was off the roster and found myself back in the minor leagues as a coach . . . teaching young athletes who were better players than I was how to play the game. And that's when I finally discovered the real talent God gave me, the one thing that I was really good at—teaching.

"I not only taught baseball as a coach, but since 1970 I've also been a high-school history and social studies teacher in the off seasons. And whether I'm in the classroom teaching world history to high-school kids or on the baseball field teaching rookies about baseball, as long as I keep doing the best teaching job I can with the talent God gave me, I have no reason to worry about anything.

"I've learned that God made something good, something special in each of us. I also finally figured out that worrying about games that were already over was taking God's gift and wasting it on *what might have been*. What's really important is to treasure and develop the gift I have for being a teacher and a coach, and God will take care of the rest.

"I live by what I call 'The Ten Day Plan.' If there's any way a problem will change or go away in ten days then, for heaven's sake, I don't waste precious time even thinking about it, let alone worrying about it.

"Every spring I get a case of hay fever so bad that I wish I could pull my eyes out and scratch 'em. But instead of worrying about it I say to myself, 'Is this situation going to be the same in ten days?' There's a good chance my eyes will be just fine in ten days, so why worry about it now?

"Or when two of my best players were both out on the injured list by the fifth week of the season, I refused to worry about it. I just said, 'Will they still be out in ten days?' The answer was 'No, they probably won't.' And you know what? Practically everything is either solved or at least gets better within ten days.

"So you see, the reason I was able to keep going when the Brewers fell from the mountaintop after that incredible 13–0 season starter, even during our twelve-game losing streak, was knowing that God gave each of us, including my players, a unique talent. If I work to my capacity as a coach and my players work to their capacity as a team, then we'll win those games. If we don't, we'll lose. If we lose often enough some of us will lose our jobs, including me. But that just means either I'm not measuring up to the talents God gave me or it means I'm not the right person for this particular job at this particular time. So then it'll be time to move on, to do the next thing that God has in store for me.

"The difference between a winning streak and a losing streak is not how much worrying I do, but what I do with that precious gift of goodness and talent that God gave me in the first place. The fact that the Milwaukee Brewers is the only team in baseball history to win and lose a dozen games in a row in the same season just proves that from one extreme to the other, win or lose, up or down, the human spirit is capable of incredible change. Worrying about changes that might have been or about what might happen in the future won't change anything. Hard work and faith in your unique talent is what gets the job done."

Life's Too Short to Be Lived in Stages

ON A SEVENTY-DEGREE October Monday, eight women of various ages and stages take the day off work and drive away from the city to a place called Scuppernong Springs in Wisconsin's rolling, forested Kettle Moraine. After hiking to the point in the woods where natural underground springs bubble up through the sand and form the beginning of the Scuppernong Creek, we women snuggle up to towering gold-leafed trees and pull tablets out of our backpacks. We are on what has been billed as a "Write-Hike."

Before my pen hits paper I study each woman as she sits among the trees and rocks near the stream. Flannery O'Connor once said, "The writer should never be ashamed of staring. There is nothing that doesn't require his attention." And so, I stare at the women.

I know one woman quite well. Judy. She organized the Write-Hike as part of her writing studio, where many of us go to learn and teach our craft. I've been introduced to four of the other women once or twice during the previous six months; the other two I've never seen until this day. In a cathedral of towering trees I wonder about their lives, about where they've been and where they're going, and about the stages of life in general.

A clever someone once said that life is made up of seven stages: spills, drills, thrills, bills, ills, pills and wills. I write those seven words on my tablet, then look around at the others. I wonder, *Are spills only for toddlers and drills for young children? Do we have to be old to take pills for our ills and worry about wills? Are thrills and bills only for yuppies and middle-agers? Where do we eight women fit into the stages of life?*

STAGE ONE—SPILLS

Just then Jean stands up to take a closer look at the bubbles in the foot-deep stream. She steps onto a grassy, boggy area, takes a spill and sinks into muddy, sandy goo. We watch Jean as she tries to work her hiking boots out of the mud. It's fun to watch. Finally, Christine grabs Jean's hand and pulls hard to break the suction of mud around Jean's ankles. Spills are fun.

STAGE TWO—DRILLS

Sometimes it seems that life's drills are never over. Today it's writing exercises. Judy tells us to use our five senses to describe these woods. And so I write:

> As birds chirp, caw, tweet or whatever it is birds do when their woods are invaded by eight women, the smell of fresh earth mingles with the feel of this mossy, leaf-crunch, drizzly day. A curtain opens at the end of the ravine and the sun bursts forth through the drizzle like a chariot in a Ben Hur movie.

As the drill continues, I wonder, *Have I ever seen the beginning of a stream before? Have I ever come this close to the beginning of something so magnificently ongoing and good?*

STAGE THREE—THRILLS

We continue our hike, *ooh*ing and *aah*ing over the perfect splendor of these Technicolor woods on this fall day. How glorious it is to escape the city, the workplace and our families, if only for eight hours.

At each turn in the path I catch my breath at a scene more spectacular than the last. Are these the thrills of my life as I approach fifty? I pick up my step to walk with Carol, an interesting, forty-something single parent who works as a massage therapist. In answer to my question, she explains her forty-dollar total body massage. I pledge to make room for one in my budget.

STAGE FOUR—BILLS

Judy worries too much about bills. I don't worry enough. That's because Judy's the boss of the writing studio and bosses have to worry about bills. But the thing about Judy is she would lug her favorite people to places of perfection like this even if she had to say, "Forget the bills. I'm just not going to worry anymore." The woods and this stream are, after all, free.

Caroline mentions that at age thirty she's living on her savings while she spends a year as an intern actress. Bills are scary for Caroline.

STAGE FIVE—ILLS

I'm sure, as I look at these women, that we all have ills. We go to bed at night with them or we wake up with them. Aches, pains, stress, sickness, disease, something gone *kapooey* with our bodies. It happens.

Today, Bobbie's cane reminds me. But in spite of her back problems, Bobbie's fifty-something-year-old spirit is so much bigger than her cane that she forces me to take a look at my own life and future health. I decide that I will walk these woods with a sack lunch when I'm ninety.

STAGE SIX—PILLS

Just like the leaves in these woods, pills—the things that make us well—come in all sizes, shapes, colors and textures. As I finish the first fifty years of my life, I pop vitamin E to keep my skin as pliable as silly putty, vitamin C to keep away the colds, calcium to keep my bones from bending into an old woman shape, vitamin A because . . . I'm not sure why, and ibuprofen to ease the arthritic ache that slinks and slithers into my fingers, toes and elbows during the night. The best part of these pills is I can pop 'em all into my mouth at once, gulp them down with one giant slurp of juice, and be on my way.

STAGE SEVEN—WILLS

I have one. And, yes, it's fair. Everything to be divided equally among my four children. Everything? Who's to get my crock collection? Twenty-nine crocks. Tiny little crocks, half-gallon butter crocks, ten-, fifteen-, even a twenty-five-gallon crock. All antiques worth hundreds, perhaps a thousand dollars altogether. Who will get my crocks? And Grandmother's pocket watch, inscribed, "To Minta Pearl on her graduation, June 1899." Who will get Grandmother's watch? The photo albums, so well organized my friends and family think I have a Felix Unger personality when it comes to photo albums. Neatly arranged photo albums from my high-school days to this very day. Dozens upon dozens of them all arranged in perfect date order on shelves made especially for my photo albums, each one labeled on the binding by date of course. If they divide the photo albums, each child will get only twenty-five percent of my life and theirs. Twenty-five percent is not enough. Who will get my photo albums? Wills. I must put mine in better order.

As we cross an old footbridge and move toward the lake, I line up with Mary, another massage therapist. After a few minutes I ask, "I've never understood the question, 'If a tree falls in the woods and there's no one around to hear it, does it make a sound?'"

Mary says it has something to do with quantum physics. She starts to explain, but my creative right brain doesn't understand any of it. But I do understand that as we come to the edge of the woods I've gained a whole new insight into Mary's intelligence and sense of humor.

Just then, Mary and Caroline spot a playground and race to the swings. As they pump higher and higher, I think about the stages of life and how it is that we women can flit from one stage to another and back again. I think once more about Grandmother's watch and about redoing that will of mine. As I walk toward the campfire, I decide that I'll do it someday when I'm ninety and it's too cold to walk in these woods. For now it's time for roasted marshmallows, swinging on swings, getting to know these women better and enjoying the final hours of a very righteous Write-Hike.

Life's Too Short
to Be on Overload

LIFE IS FULL OF WARNINGS. Thunderstorm or tornado warnings flash across our TV screens to allow us time to prepare for bad weather. Road signs—Slippery When Wet, Winding Road, Detour Ahead—give us the message to proceed with caution.

Our bodies give us warning signs. Tiredness, discomfort, weight loss, weight gain, shortness of breath, irritability and pain are signs telling us to proceed with caution, visit a doctor, or change the pace.

One time a woman told me about her hectic life. Her full-time job, the social activities her husband's career demanded of her, the responsibility of her three children, caring for their home, food and clothing, her involvement in two church groups and a professional group, all spread her time so thin that she had nothing left for herself. Every minute of every day, weekends included, was preprogrammed and the family calendar looked like something prepared by the White House social secretary.

Her health suffered. Tiredness, depression, lingering guilt, anxiety and constant criticism became a way of life. Finally, she realized she was on *overload*.

At the urging of her friends, family and psychotherapist,

the woman took a week's vacation and made a list of all the things she wanted to do in her life, not the ones she felt she *had* to do. She discovered that spending time alone with her husband and children was very important to her. She also liked her job, even though it didn't leave much time for cleaning the house, cooking and doing laundry.

Rather than back down on her teaching career, she gave up the job of superwoman. She hired a woman to clean her house every other week, started taking her husband's shirts to the dry cleaner, made plans for the family to eat out twice a week, and shared the rest of the kitchen responsibilities with her husband and children, who discovered that figuring out new menus, grocery shopping and puttering in the kitchen was interesting, if not downright fun when they did it together.

Once that woman was able to let go of the traditional roles of woman/wife/mother and concentrate on those things that made use of her talents as a teacher, her warmth as a friend and a spouse and her love of mothering all returned big time. Her life became fulfilling and her good health returned. She found time to smell the flowers at the botanical garden, enjoy sunsets and nights out with her husband alone, take leisurely walks by herself, fly kites with her younger son, play piano duets with her daughter, and attend her older son's baseball games. Best of all, she was able to bask in the knowledge that she didn't have to be or do everything in order to be successful.

Is your life too hectic? These days that's like asking someone if they breathe very often. Of course our lives are too hectic! I have to admit my hectic life has slowed down considerably since my children went to college, graduated and started their own lives in distant towns. It also helped when I quit my job in 1992 to stay home and do what I love more than anything . . . plunk away at the computer, writing books.

Being single probably makes my life less hectic too. Although I do have a nagging feeling that I don't want to grow old alone, and looking for Mr. Perfect is a bit nerve-wracking at times. At least for now, there are no arguments about leaving the bedroom window open or who burned the toast or why the grass hasn't been mowed for a month or why there's a scratch on the car or who left the newspaper on the floor . . . well, you get the picture. Life, for me, is simple and relatively stress-free. And I, too, am happy, healthy and content.

If your life isn't stress-free, perhaps you need to eliminate some things and trim down the importance of others. Perhaps you need to stop feeling guilty if you hire someone else to do some of the work for you. Call a family meeting and explain the new division of property, *property* being cleaning, cooking, laundry and yard work.

My dear friend Shirley Winston tells about the day she called such a meeting. "It was the day of my great fit, still referred to thirty years later as 'The Day Mom Threw Her Fit.'

"Wally and I were both teaching full time, but he and Scott [their only child] always managed to have time every weekend for hunting, fishing, exploring, canoeing, camping, and hanging out in the garage, basement or backyard. You name it, they were the great outdoor pioneers. In the meantime, on weekends especially, I was schlepping to the grocery store, running errands, cooking, cleaning, doing laundry, running the entire house. Finally I had it . . . *my big fit*. I blurted out my complaints and woes with more anger than I'd ever exposed to the world, let alone to Wally and Scott, and then went on strike immediately thereafter. It didn't take my husband and son long to discover that part of their leisure time was, from that moment on, going to involve some of the cooking, cleaning and laundry. I look back on 'The Day Mom Threw Her Fit' and see it as the turning point in our lives. From then on we were all much happier."

I heard once that if the mother in a family is happy, then everybody's happy. If Mom is unhappy, watch out! There's a potential land mine around every corner.

If today's the day your family chore list is going to be redistributed and your lives are going to become more satisfying, let me offer one bit of advice. When you call that family meeting, start by telling each person in the family how much you love and appreciate them. Diffuse the mood of gloom and doom with positive statements. Then get down to work and have your fit. Well, you don't really need to have a fit, per se. Fits are generally reserved for those families whose distribution of family-related work has really gotten out of hand. You may just quietly need to figure out positive ways you can all work together to make the whole family function like a well-oiled machine, with time for each of you to smell the brownies baking, flowers growing, fresh air blowing.

Personally, I think life is too short not to have one great fit. Like Wally and Shirley, you'll be talking and laughing about it for generations.

Life's Too Short
to Send your Kids
Door to Door

AFTER RAISING FOUR wonderfully diverse children who have participated in nearly every activity possible during grade, middle and high school, I have one thing to say: Praise the Lord my fund-raising days are over!

Now don't get your socks in a bunch. I'm not against the idea of helping organizations. I just hate being asked to buy something for ten dollars that's barely worth five dollars when only two dollars of the ten dollars actually go into the child's school fund.

How would we feel if, instead of asking churchgoers for a monetary donation each Sunday when the basket is passed, we were asked to buy pizza, cookies, candy bars, coupon books, window stickers, greeting cards, gift wrap, household trinkets, tacky decorations, popcorn and citrus fruit, ad infinitum every Sunday so the pastor and the staff could pay the church bills?

Well, that's what the schools do, public and private. They fund-raise us to death. Not only do most of our dollars end up in the fat pockets of the fund-raising companies that provide the substandard products at an inflated cost, but we have the added insult that every time our child begs a friend, relative or neighbor to buy their usually tacky overpriced fund-raising products, we immediately become obligated to purchase the same amount of substandard products from the children of those friends, neighbors and relatives who bought from our children. It's a vicious cycle that costs us double in the long run.

After bellyaching about fund-raising for more than twenty years, since my oldest child was six years old and selling gaudy gizmos and what-have-you, my youngest child listened carefully when I told him a true story about his deceased father.

Years ago Andrew's dad was a high-school band director and director of Milwaukee's Lake Band, a youth band for kids from many different high schools. One year Harold had enough of futile fund-raisers. He went to his friends in the media and asked them to publicize his *one-and-only* fund-raising event for the year. The local newspapers, radio and TV all cooperated and spread the word. Harold needed something like twenty thousand dollars for the band trips and activities for the year. He said he would send his kids, dressed in their band uniforms, out into the community for two hours on a Sunday afternoon. Each student would carry a bucket for donations. No candy, no pizza, no coupon books, no fruit. Just a bucket for cold hard cash. Harold promised the community that there would be no more fund-raising that year, other than that one two-hour door-to-door event. He also told them that if they didn't raise the entire twenty thousand dollars that afternoon they would only go on the number of band trips for which they did have enough money. When the kids returned to the school, they not only had enough money for the entire year's worth of activities, they had enough for half of the following year, too.

The day I told Andrew that story about his father, he sat down at his computer and wrote the following letter:

Dear _____,

Every year the Oak Creek High School Band goes on a big trip in the spring. Each student must raise $450 to go on the trip. Of course the band provides lots of fund-raisers. All year long I could be approaching you numerous times to see if you want to buy the useless fund-raising items that the OCHS Band offers.

Imagine this: Late September. (*Ding dong.*) Hello! How would you like to buy a coupon book from me? It costs ten dollars, but only four dollars actually go into my band trip account. Two weeks later. (*Ding dong.*) Hello! How would you like to buy Hardee's dollars? They're just like regular dollar bills, but you can only spend them at Hardee's. Each one costs a dollar, but only forty cents for each one I sell actually go into my fund account. Three weeks later. (*Ding dong.*) Hello! How would you like to buy a magazine subscription? You can subscribe to hundreds of magazines, but only about forty percent of what it costs actually goes into my fund account. Three weeks later. (*Ding dong.*) Hello! How would you like to buy a crate of oranges or grape-fruit? They're fresh from Florida, and they'll last you from now until spring. (Yeah, right.) The thing is, only a few bucks actually go into my band trip fund account.

One week later. (*Ding dong.*) Hello! How would you like to sponsor me in my band's bowl-a-thon? You can give me money for bowling. Isn't that a great idea? And you know what? I'm also going to ask if you want to come and watch me bowl! Yes, it's a great way to spend a Sunday afternoon . . . watching a bunch of teenagers who think bowling is nerdy bowl for the band. Six weeks later. (*Ding dong.*) Hello! Is it just me or do you need a kringle? Well, I just happen to be selling them for my band trip. I know it's spring, but you can always use a kringle. They're high in fat and sugar, and they cost an arm and a leg. However, not even half of what the total cost is goes into my band trip fund account.

Well, by now you're probably thinking, *Wow, that Andrew is sure something! He loves me so much that he's not going to ask me to buy useless junk like that.* You're right. I do appreciate you. And I'm not going to ask you to buy one thing this year! But if you would like to help me get to Washington, D.C., a small donation would be great. Whatever you want to give. At least you'll know that whatever you choose to donate, one hundred percent goes into my band trip account. Thanks a lot for listening, and I hope I'll see you soon. But I promise . . . it won't be to sell you anything!

Much love,

Andrew

Family, friends and neighbors sent checks to Andrew with notes applauding his creativity. He received enough donations for the whole trip, plus some extra for spending money. What he learned from this experience is that the Bible verse "Ask, and you will be given what you ask for"

(Matthew 7:7, TLB) works not just for getting our prayers answered and problems solved, but in finding practical solutions to everyday earthly needs as well.

When the little girl next door asks me to buy boxes of cookies for $2.75 each, I give her a five-dollar donation instead. One hundred percent of that goes into her individual troop fund. I would have to buy twelve boxes of cookies for her troop to net five dollars since only about forty cents a box goes to the individual troops. Twelve boxes at $2.75 each would have cost me thirty-three dollars.

Direct donations work for our churches. They can work for our schools, too. One thing I know, it works for me.

Life's Too Short
to Say No to your Heart

I HARDLY RECOGNIZED the voice on the phone as that of my youngest son Andrew, a sophomore at Arizona State University.

"Mom," he whispered in obvious distress, "I'm in the hospital, really sick. I can't talk. Pain's too bad. Can you come out?"

I talked to the emergency room doctor, who said they were treating him for food poisoning or flu. After talking to Andrew's surgeon in our hometown, whose diagnosis was different, my pounding heart felt like a lead weight sinking into the pit of my chest. "Sounds like complications from the surgery he had last year," he said.

An hour later Andrew was taken out of the ER and admitted to the hospital. The rest of the day I was on the phone with the attending physician, the nurse, his doctor at home, his ASU student health physician, my other three children, various friends and some of Andrew's teachers. It was final exam week and they needed to be notified.

Should I drop everything and fly out to be with my son? If I could get on a flight I could only stay three days, because for six months I'd been scheduled as the keynote speaker at the statewide PTA convention in central Wisconsin and simply could not back out of that at such a late date.

Was I being too smothering to rush to him? He was, after all, twenty years old and had weathered two other hospitalizations alone in Arizona during the previous school year. But Andrew asked again, twice, that day, "Mom, can't you please come out?"

Oh, how I wanted to be there with him. I wanted to connect his Wisconsin surgeon with the new doctors in the hospital eighteen hundred miles from home. I wanted to be his advocate and see that his care ran smoothly. Most of all I wanted to hug my son and sit by his side.

But my conscience stung. One nurse said he was definitely not in acute danger and would be fine without me. Then I remembered I was having fifteen to twenty women at my home for my SWILL group (Southeastern Wisconsin Interesting Ladies League) on one of the nights I'd be gone. Plus I had two other commitments during those three days that I'd have to cancel.

Would I be babying him by going? Should I go? Should I stay? Would he rest better if I left him to the care of the doctors and nurses out there?

It was agony that whole day. I called my other children again. Should I go? Should I stay? Can I afford it? Does it make sense to fly out and rent a car to be there for three days? Would it help or hinder Andrew's recovery with me hovering over him?

I got a huge headache. My muscles tightened around my neck and shoulders as I tried to decide what to do, what to do.

By 9:00 PM the tension was unbearable. I had to decide by ten o'clock so I could make the airline arrangements, call a friend for a ride to the airport, call another friend to host the SWILL meeting, arrange for another friend to pick up the salad I'd made for the next day's luncheon, prepare my speech for the following Saturday and pack. My head throbbed. Should I go or stay home and call him every few hours?

I called his night nurse and agonized with her. She said, "He's getting a powerful pain medication and three other drugs by IV and he's comfortable. Physically he's being taken care of . . . but . . ." her voice softened, "emotionally, I don't know. He seems very depressed."

Click. That was it. Emotionally, my son needed me. Decision made, I called my friends who would step in for me during the next three days. I packed a bag, called Andrew to tell him I'd be there at nine o'clock the next morning, prepared my speech for the following Saturday, set the alarm for 5:00 AM, and went to bed at midnight.

The instant I made the decision I felt a sense of peace, anticipation and joy at my pending eighteen-hundred-mile trip. I'd be with my son in a matter of hours. My headache left, shoulder muscles relaxed and at last I felt like a woman with a purpose, a goal, a wonderful motherhood adventure about to begin.

I learned that the difference between stressful agony and everlasting peace and purpose is the result of one thing: *making the decision.*

Make the decision. That's all there is to it. Simply

decide, one way or the other, and the rest is chocolate syrup on the ice cream.

Andrew's face lit up like a firefly at night when I arrived. After a day and a half of more drugs and mother hugs, intense rest and the stuff a mom does best, Andrew was released from the hospital, giving us a day and a half of fun together.

I will never agonize over a decision for so long ever again. If you've got one to make, make it and go from there. Believe me, the rest is sledding downhill on fresh powder snow. Pure joy and purpose with pizzazz.

Chapter Seven

Leisure
Loop-de-Loops

I decided quite a few years ago that having time to play and explore and travel and think and read and create is more about what life is all about than being stressed out with too many pressures, meetings, quotas, responsibilities and an ulcer-causing daily list of things that must be done at the office. When I gave up my job in 1992 and the daily pressures that went with it, I put on my favorite cotton knit casual togs and fell in love with working at home.

Let's see. Do I want to go to my writing room downstairs and crank out a story for my next book, or do I want to make brownies and invite a friend over for a tea party? Hmm. Some days I choose work because I'm doing work that I love. But other days it's tea party time, or time to visit my folks three hours away in Illinois, or time for a bike ride or a walk along beautiful Lake Michigan. Or an afternoon of painting jars, a hobby I developed in the mid-1990s. I love my life! I have time with my loved ones, time to sing and dance and shout and stretch, and time just to enjoy this amazing world full of diverse people, places and things.

Excuse me, it's time for a cup of tea.

Life's Too Short
to Sell your Airboat

"YOU BOUGHT WHAT?" whooped my usually tiny-voiced mother, who kept the family budget balanced to the last penny. "You bought an airplane engine? Let me get this straight. You bought an airplane engine and propeller, but no airplane, right?"

Dad stroked his chin. "Yup. A beauty, too. Sixty-five horsepower Lycoming engine. It's on a boat. Boat needs some work, though. It's called an airboat, Lucy. You're gonna love it. It's a flat-bottomed boat. We'll be able to cruise the backwaters of Rock River and fish in five or six inches of water."

Mom shook her head and muttered something about preferring to hook her fish at the local Piggly Wiggly.

That was the summer of 1955.

Imagine a boat so flat on the bottom it could fly across deep river waters or skim across wet grass. Imagine a boat so noisy that it could scare whole schools of fish into instant retreat . . . or so quiet you could hear a tadpole flip out of the water ten feet away. A boat so versatile that in the winter one could attach runners to the bottom and blast across a frozen body of water toward an ice fishing hole.

Well, I didn't have to imagine it. I grew up with it. The

Beast, as we sometimes called the airboat, was built from a little of this and a little of that. Bits and pieces. Old junk, new paint. Discards and treasures.

A few days after Dad introduced his new acquisition to Mom, he came home with two wide seats that he had unbolted from an abandoned school bus in the junkyard.

"Seats are in great shape!" he beamed to Mother. "Red leather. Not a hole or a scratch on 'em. I just have to cut 'em down a bit so they're not quite so tall. One's a two-seater, the other's a three-seater. The airboat will easily hold five people across."

Mother said something encouraging like, "Be still, my fluttering heart."

Dad spent the next few months getting the fourteen-foot-long, six-foot-wide, boxy-looking boat into shape. He built two large four-foot-tall rudders on the back end, telling Mom that two rudders would be much better than one because with two rudders the airflow from the pro-peller would provide a full blast of air with which to direct the boat.

Mother just nodded, probably figuring that his stint as a fighter pilot during World War II had left her husband with permanent airplane engine mania.

Next, Dad rebuilt the hull with all new oak framing and half-inch marine plywood on the bottom and sides. The front was bent up in a streamlined shape so there'd be very little drag. He covered the hull with fiberglass. A slick machine, without a doubt.

Finally, he fixed up the joystick, so it could control

both the engine and the steering mechanism in one easy wrist action. The pilot simply had to pull the control stick back to go fast, forward to go slower or stop, and right or left to go right or left. A two-year-old could drive that boat.

After a snazzy paint job—gray/green on the hull and bright red on the back end, including silver diagonal racing stripes from top to bottom on the twin rudders—the Rock River *Beast* was ready for action.

"Hey, Dad," I squealed in my most excited ten-year-old voice, "it really does look like a boat! When can we take it out?"

"Not until I figure out how to keep your hands out of the propeller," Dad mused as he walked through his collection of junk stacked neatly out behind the garage.

Since the bus seats were only a couple feet from the violent airplane propeller, he needed a propeller guard to keep human appendages, hats and fishing supplies out of the prop.

Dad made a circular propeller guard out of half-inch electrical conduit. He covered the conduit with heavy wire mesh. The contraption kept everything out of the boat's airplane propeller. If OSHA (Occupational Safety and Health Administration) had been around then, they'd have been proud of my dad's safety measures.

Airboat complete, Dad's creative genius continued as he designed and built a three-wheeled trailer to haul it. The tires were short and fat, single-engine airplane tires, of course.

The day before Dad launched the airboat for the first

time on Rock River in Rock Falls, Illinois, was the last weekend of peace and quiet the residents who lived along the river enjoyed. When that *Beast* hit the water with its mighty airplane engine blasting, the sound bounced off the shore, magnified itself a couple of times and echoed back along the surface of the water, creating what sounded like a swarm of B-52 bombers.

Every weekend for the next few summers my mother, younger brother and I slid onto those bus seats and covered our ears while Dad hand-popped the prop. I remember yelling with delight into the deafening roar that swallowed our words like a heavy blanket. We were off and blaring as the boat's broad flat surface slapped hard against the waves.

Before long, folks who lived along the river either dashed to their living room picture windows to wave or jerked themselves outside to view the thundering little red and green *Beast* as it skimmed and bounced across the water. We were a sight. Hair and jackets flying straight back toward the propeller and banana-sized grins on our faces. We owned the river by the sheer force of our sound.

As a somewhat laid-back sport fisherman, Dad soon discovered all the advantages of having a flat-bottomed boat. We could explore the back swamp areas that were often only five to ten inches deep. With the engine off, the only sound we could hear as we drifted lazily along was that of an occasional fish popping out of the water. I was never quite sure if it was really that quiet out there in the backwaters or if my ears were just temporarily out of whack once Dad shut off the screaming *Beast*.

The fish—large mouth bass, channel cats, bullheads, fatheads and crappie—were mostly outnumbered by over-sized carp. The carp thrived in those calm, shallow, sun-warmed backwaters. They thrived, that is, until Dad decided to teach us to fish in a rather unconventional fashion with the airboat as our launching pad.

It was simple fishing. No rod, no reel, no bait. Just Dad's homemade five-foot-long spear with five sharp prongs at the end. All we had to do was wait until one of those fat, lazy, backwater carp wiggled by, stand up quietly and throw the spear into the fish's back with one swift clean snap of the wrist.

During spawning season we'd see dozens of carp of all sizes wiggling around the shallow backwaters of the muddy Rock. We sure didn't need a fish finder back then!

In his attempt to increase our catches, Dad also bought a short, primitive fiberglass bow. The arrow had fishing line attached to it, so it wouldn't be lost in the mud if we missed our target. Trying to catch a fish with a bow and arrow was not only a challenge, it was a sport that definitely had its pitfalls. More than once the shooter lost her balance and fell into gooey waste-deep mud the consistency of face cream. But when you came up with a five-pound carp on the end of your arrow, the feeling of accomplishment made the mud bath worthwhile.

I remember taking my favorite bamboo pole along on the airboat a few times, but the dough balls I hastily created from the sandwiches Mother packed somehow didn't entice those carp critters enough to take advantage of my offer.

Actually, if you want to know the truth, we weren't really terribly serious when it came to fishing from the airboat. Dad said the carp that thrived in those backwaters were scavenger fish that had a muddy flavor and were too bony to eat anyway. So we were never too disappointed if our day on the river sent us home without a fish to our name.

But that doesn't mean we didn't constantly look for fish, because we did. The main sport, instead of catching them and frying them for supper, was to watch intently for the familiar V-shaped wake each fish created in the shallow waters. Then Dad would speed up the boat and cruise right over the top of those big shiny-backed beauties. It didn't hurt the fish, since the boat was flat on the bottom, but we'd laugh ourselves silly knowing that if fish had ears they were probably wondering whether the world was coming to an end when our monster noise contraption slid over the tops of their backs.

The truth of the matter is that our hunting/fishing instincts were often abandoned at the dock and our natural resource/wildlife preservation instincts took over as soon as we hit the backwaters and shut off the *Beast*'s engine. Blue and white herons, dancing like ballerinas on their long skinny legs, paraded in front of us somewhat proudly as we whispered in the weeds. Wood ducks and mallards entertained us at sea level; red-wing blackbirds flitted from tree to tree on the backwater islands; and sometimes a skein of Canadian geese provided encore entertainment from the clouds.

Even the animals seemed to consider our silent contraption nonthreatening as we watched muskrats, beavers, wood-chucks and water snakes slide around in the water and on the small islands near our primitive observation deck.

I remember one time in particular when it was neither fowl, fish, nor mammal that provided our most entertaining moment. It was my mother. Dad was showing off his boat-ing skills to out-of-state relatives when he headed the air-boat back to a lagoon and zoomed onto a low peninsula of grass and water lilies. The airboat started sashaying on a mud bank, and when Dad jerked the throttle back, to pick up speed and pulled a fast ninety-degree turn, my mother, who was perched on the starboard edge of the bus seats, was thrown clear out of the boat.

Once we got off the mud slick and hit the water, the *Beast*, now cruising at top thirty-five-mile-an-hour speed, was actually blasting over the water, not through it, slap-ping the waves hard. That noise, plus the deafening sound of the airplane engine, prevented me from getting Dad's attention right away. It was two hundred or three hundred feet later before Dad finally caught on to why I was waving my arms like a bird in take-off. He slowed down the engine so he could hear me tell him almost hysterically that dur-ing his circus maneuvers on the mud slick Mother had fallen out of the boat and was back there somewhere up to her waist in mud, hollering her fool head off.

I don't remember how long it was before Mom rode in the airboat again, but I can still see her, clear as day, arms waving like a crazy woman and mad as a wet rooster because Dad didn't even know she was missing!

The airboat held hundreds of people in its lap over the years. A couple times every summer Dad took the whole group of local grade-school nuns for a ride. From the bank all you could see was a blur of black habits with their veils tied down. Heaven forbid that the sheer force of wind from the propeller suck off one of those veils. I often wondered what would have happened had I discovered at the tender age of ten that nuns really did have hair under those long black habits. At least I experienced the thrill of knowing firsthand that a nun who constantly fingered her Rosary and who might rap your desk with her ruler at the drop of a hat during a spelling test, was also a fun human being who could laugh like a hyena on your dad's airboat on the weekend.

When my parents' friends had relatives visiting from out of town, they always called up to collect that "promised ride." The old airboat was the best standby for proving to out-of-towners that Rock River Valley in northern Illinois certainly had its unique attractions and that fishing for carp with a spear or cruising over their shallow wakes was more fun than fishing with a two-hundred-dollar graphite rod from a *real* fishing boat.

During the winters when the muddy Rock River froze over, Dad converted the airboat into an iceboat by adding steel runners clamped under the hull. On the ice, the red and green monster chewed up the freezing cold air and snow into its mighty prop and blasted it back into the faces of those riding behind on sleds, toboggans and saucers.

Even on calm days the airplane propeller created such a

violent blizzard that the best way to ride behind without getting a frostbitten face was to sit on the sleds backward. As the iceboat slipped sideways and in circles, and with all kinds of things and people riding behind backward, it was a hilarious spectator sport for the folks on the riverbank.

One extremely hot summer the airboat proved to be the grandest invention in town without even being near the water. One night when the temperature reached a humid 101 degrees, our un-air-conditioned house was suffocating. No one could get to sleep, so at about 2:00 AM, out of sheer desperation, Dad backed the airboat up to the dining room window and popped the prop. Within ten seconds the blast from that airplane propeller swooshed through the house—dusting all the tabletops and tumbling furniture doilies—and provided a blast of arctic air that gave us back our sweet dispositions.

We saw some of the neighbors' lights pop on during our noisy blast, terrified, no doubt, that an airplane was about to land on their roofs. But after a few minutes of what sounded like a Strategic Air Command red alert, Dad shut off the engine and we all slept quite blissfully.

That old airboat provided the best times of my childhood. But after fifteen years of airboat fun, Dad tired of the noisy, fast, furious *Beast*. He gave it to his older brother who added it to his collection of junk and it never saw water again. Shortly thereafter Dad started collecting 250-gallon oil drums for his next project, a pontoon boat for his retirement years.

Dad welded ten of those oil drums together, built a

large 336-square-foot deck floor, then added an elaborate *African Queen*-type wooden pitched roof on the back half, complete with a birdhouse and an American flag. A dozen lawn chairs, a grill for river cookouts and an elaborate captain's chair finished off the comforts-of-home decor.

From 1981 to 1998, when Dad gave the pontoon boat to the Rock River Development Authority, my dad and stepmom Bev spent their retired summers floating ever so calmly and quietly up and down the mighty muddy Rock River. Sure, we had plenty of relaxing fun during those years in the eighties and nineties, but none of us ever speared a carp, pulled a sled or cooled off the house with the pontoon boat. *Ah* yes, I do miss that *Beast*. And when I think back to my childhood, I have to say that life's definitely too short to ever sell your airboat.

Life's Too Short
Not to Love Rock and Roll

AS A MEMBER OF the first graduating class of the baby
boomer generation, I've never really been sure what to
think about all the fuss about rock music. Ever since the
1950s, rock and roll has been given a bum rap. It's been
called a nemesis, the moral corrupter, the devil's music, the
cause of teenage demise.

Well, maybe some of the lyrics *have* caused some young
people to flip out temporarily as moral deviants but, generally speaking, my opinion of rock and roll is this: It's got a
good beat and it's fun to dance to. But I have to admit, I've
been confused about the issue ever since I interviewed
Chubby Checker in 1984. He told me he was going straight
to hell for singing rock and roll, but because he liked it so
much he had to do it anyway. I've been bemused about rock
and roll since 1985 when my five-year-old told me his
favorite song was, "I Love Rock and Roll, Put Another Dime
in the Jukebox, Baby."

I grew up in the fifties and sixties with rock and roll
music pushing me every step of the way. Every day at
Newman Central Catholic High School in Sterling, Illinois,
the Sisters of Loretto plugged in the jukebox after lunch
and let the girls fast-dance in the cafeteria while the boys

played basketball in the gym. We rocked, we rolled. We swished around the high-school cafeteria to the likes of Paul Anka, Fabian, Chubby Checker, Frankie Avalon, Elvis, Sha Na Na, The Shirelles and the Everly Brothers. We liked the beat and only listened to the words of such songs as "Teen Angel" and "Patches" at the high-school mixers on Friday nights because they had stories to tell . . . sad, melodramatic, tear-jerking tales that usually ended in the tragic death of one of the lovers.

We loved rock and roll because it opened up the flood of emotions that we teenagers were experiencing. We loved it because those wonderful three-chord beats were so powerful you just had to get up and dance. I've always thought those nuns were smart to let us dance during lunch hour. We used our pent-up energy and then settled down quite nicely during afternoon classes.

The years passed. Marriage, children, career. Suddenly we were mothers with teenagers of our own and our children were being socked with a load of guilt about *today's* rock music. Religious leaders, the media, school administrators and parents who had actually taken the time to listen to the words of today's rock music were up in arms. Granted, some of the lyrics of the hard rock groups certainly do step beyond the bounds of decency. As parents we must protect our children from moral corruption. But do we do it by yanking away their rock music, or is it enough to teach them good moral values and hope that they really don't listen to the words, as many claim?

My real concern about rock music started that night I

interviewed Chubby Checker, the man who made the Twist the biggest dance craze since the Charleston. When I asked Chubby about his career, he caught me off-guard when he said that rock and roll music was all wrong.

The Twist King explained, "Both of my grandfathers were orthodox apostolic ministers who taught me that rock music is very wrong. Just listen to the lyrics. They're all about going to bed or booze or drugs. It's wrong. And with God it's either the right way or the wrong way. Rock music is the wrong way."

Now I was really confused. How could these statements be coming from a man who had made rock and roll his life? So I asked, "If what you're doing is so wrong, why do you keep doing it?"

Chubby Checker had just come off the stage after a highly successful concert at a big club in Wisconsin. He looked me square in the eye and said, "I'm not saved, yet I'm satisfied with my life. I love singing. I'm good at it. I feel terrific when I'm out there. But I know it's wrong, and until I repent I won't be special with God. The world is on a self-destruct course, full of sin, greed and pollution. There are no rock and roll singers in heaven."

Oh, Chubby. Didn't you see those people, young and old alike, out there dancing to your music? Older, heavy-set women who probably hadn't had any exercise in months, twistin' and smilin'. . . happy for the first time in weeks, perhaps? How can you call that simple joy sinful? I wondered.

That interview festered in my soul like a splinter that refuses to come out. Later I attended a forum in Milwaukee titled, "What's Today's Rock Music Doing to Our Kids?" The panelists included a disc jockey, a priest who talked about the good side of rock music every week on a half-hour radio show, the head of a "Positive Alternatives for Youth" program, an adolescent psychotherapist, and an author of a book about rock and roll lyrics.

What I learned from the panel was that even though teens are bombarded with messages from the media (CDs, TV, radio, videos and commercials) about irresponsible sex, drugs, booze and abuse, teens still make prudent judgments about their sexuality with the help of solid family support and open communication in the home with parents and peers.

One thing is certain: Suggestive lyrics to songs have been around a long time, long before rock even heard of roll. The forties and fifties gave us Nat King Cole's "They Tried to Tell Us We're Too Young." They were young, but they did it anyway. Andy William's "Strangers in the Night." They weren't strangers for long. Fats Domino's "I Found My Thrill on Blueberry Hill" makes you wonder just how big that thrill was. In 1964, the Drifters' "Under the Boardwalk" was about a secret place for a secret love affair.

The priest on that panel said that rock music is the expression of all of our emotions, set musically to the beat that happens to be in vogue. Whether it's the fifties sound with its simple three-chord arrangement; the sixties revolutionary sound and bubble-gum type music; the seventies with its studio sound, beefed-up arrangements and the disco craze; the eighties with the huge studio and synthe-sized sound; or the nineties and beyond conglomeration of everything computerized and electronic . . . rock music is simply moods, situations and attitudes set to music.

But what about the modern trend of teen suicides? The headlines all over the country screaming, "Are Rock Lyrics Words to Die By?" A survey conducted by the *Milwaukee Journal* in the early nineties discovered that most young people saw nothing wrong with rock music lyrics. Fourteen percent of the youths surveyed said the lyrics had a good effect, twenty percent said they had a bad effect, and sixty-two percent said there was no effect from lyrics . . . probably because as most teens said, "We never listen to the words anyway."

We'll be debating about the effect of rock music on our lives forever. In the meantime, it's certainly a good idea for parents to keep a watchful eye on how much time their children spend watching MTV and whether or not they're into some of the hardest of the hard rock groups that do promote grotesqueness in the form of drugs, perversion, profanity, prejudice, Satanism, sexual exploitation, abuse and mutilation. Certainly, we shouldn't allow our children to listen to these extremes of rock music. The easiest way to learn which groups fall into this category is to read the lyrics printed inside the CD cases. Ask store managers to make the lyrics available before CDs or tapes are purchased.

For the most part, today's rock music, especially the "Top 40" tunes, is no different than the rock and roll we baby boomers danced to in the fifties and sixties. The messages are mostly about relationships between people. And if we give our children the right messages by the way we live *our* lives, they'll survive today's rock the way we did.

I just hope I have the energy to dance to Chubby Checker's "Twist" when I'm seventy. And even if I don't, you can be sure I'll still enjoy hearing the Twist King belt it out. Personally, I think Chubby was wrong. I think there are *lots* of rock and roll singers in heaven.

Life's Too Short to Miss an Outhouse Race

MY FATHER ED KOBBEMAN, from the small town of Rock Falls in northern Illinois, is one of the all-time-great, get-it-done, do-it-now kind of guys. He still lives in the house he built himself in 1946, and it's a veritable showplace of repair and improvement. He's often out in the barn fixing things before they break, restoring antiques, building contraptions from scratch, or designing and creating amazing gadgets and gizmos.

It wasn't too surprising, then, when Dad proudly showed me his latest creation . . . the outhouse he'd built from the rough wood ripped from an old wooden crate. The traditional sun and moon were cut through the front door. The sloped roof had shake shingles. Dad had fashioned a fancy seat inside, within arm's reach, of course, of the supply of corn cobs dangling on strings. The dual-purpose Sears Roebuck catalog hung from a hook on one of the inside walls. There was even an American flag waving off the back end. It was, indeed, a fine outhouse.

Why a man, who built an all-electric home in the 1940s with a beautiful modern bathroom, would construct an outhouse in the 1990s was something of a puzzle to me. But then Dad explained that he intended to enter his creation in the Annual Rock Falls Days Outhouse Races.

To be in this grand event, one's outhouse had to have wheels. Dad took his off some old contraption he'd worked on years before, which he found in his neat-as-a-pin storage area outside the barn.

The day of the race, Dad's nephews, the outhouse racing team, arrived to load up his pride and joy into their pickup truck. The four team members, and one great-niece weighing in at under one hundred pounds who was chosen to ride in the seat inside, per race rules, were all wearing red look-alike, tank-style T-shirts. They looked so spiffy they could have been vying for a medal at the outhouse event at the summer Olympics.

The contraption arrived safely in the heart of downtown Rock Falls. In the blazing sun of that scorching June day, the five outhouse teams lined up. The four muscular nephews in charge of the Kobbeman outhouse grabbed the pole handles attached to either side of the wooden beauty and rocked ol' Bessy back and forth. Team unity solidified as the red-chested nephews chanted before their race with destiny, "Feel da rhythm, hear da rhyme, come on team, it's outhouse time!"

The starting shot rang out. The red-shirted Kobbeman clan, out in front by a foot, screeched around the markers thirty yards down the parking lot and turned 180 degrees to make their way back to the start/finish line.

Just then, disaster. The hard rubber on the wheels

started peeling off. One at a time, hardened black tires split off the wheels as old rubber gave way to new asphalt. The nephews hung on for the last few feet, barely winning the first race by sheer strength of will and brute muscle power as they lifted the outhouse off the ground, niece and all, and drag-carried her across the finish line. But now there was no hope for the second heat.

I stood there, ready to cry. My father had put so much time and talent into making what was obviously the superior outhouse, and now it was all over. Without wheels, an outhouse cannot run.

Out of the corner of my eye I saw Dad walking like a mad man away from the race. I wondered if he, too, was as disgusted with those old tires as I. *What a shame*, I thought, *to lose the contest because of some stupid old wheels.* Considering the strength and enthusiasm of his red-chested team, it was a low blow indeed.

Five minutes later I realized Dad hadn't come back. *Where is he?* I thought apprehensively. Thinking he'd gone off to the restroom at the corner tap, I suddenly realized that if he didn't get back soon he'd miss the rest of the races.

Minutes ticked by. By now my cousins were using the old standby, gray duct tape to wrap the wheels, foolishly hoping they could patch them together tight enough to at least try for the second race.

Five minutes later Dad was still nowhere to be seen. *Doggone, him*, I thought. *Where could he be? Gone off, upset at himself for using old tires on a new outhouse? How could he just leave like that? This was my dad, for crying out loud, the man who spent a great deal of my childhood teaching me to be a good sport, to enjoy life, but always to play the game fairly. And now, just because the wheels fell off his outhouse, he's acting like a poor sport? He could have at least stuck around to see if the patched-up, wobbly tires would work in the next race.*

The announcer was on the microphone telling the participants to get their outhouses lined up for the next heat. Just then Dad ran up to outhouse row clutching four brand-new wheels. He tossed me a few tools.

"Here, hold these. Hand me those needle-nose pliers," he said in his take-charge voice.

Within seconds, the nephews and Dad had that wooden, shake-shingled wonder on its back, ripping the duct tape off with the pliers, undoing rusty nuts and bolts, and attaching the brand-new wheels. It was a scene straight out of the pit at the Indy 500. Fifty seconds flat and those new wheels were in place.

The Kobbeman clan, with their new-and-improved-and-even-more-superior outhouse, won the next four races amidst plenty of good-natured hooting and hollering from the folks on the sidelines. In the ceremony that followed, Dad and his nephews and great-niece were presented with an outhouse trophy so spectacular that it could only be given to the finest of privy makers. That shiny blue and gold, two-foot-tall trophy even had a tiny little outhouse on top with the door wide open, as if to say, "Come on in, friend!"

After the presentation, photo session and lots of back slapping and congratulatory kudos from the townspeople, including the mayor, we headed home. In the car I asked Dad, "Where'd you go when you ran off like that? And where'd you get those new wheels?"

My father, who was just two months shy of his seventy-fifth birthday, took a deep breath. "Well," he said, starting slowly, then speeding up his words as he told the story, "I ran two and a half blocks to the car, unlocked it, drove two miles home like a bat out of Bangkok, ran in the house, got the key to the barn, ran out there, unlocked the barn, pulled my new lawnmower out on the grass, grabbed some tools, pulled off the first two wheels, and threw 'em in the car. Then I decided I could take the other two off downtown while the boys were puttin' the first two on the outhouse. So I lifted that lawnmower into the back end of the station wagon, then I decided that was dumb. I could take the wheels off there at home just as fast, so I lifted the lawn-mower back out of the car and unbolted the second pair of wheels, threw 'em in the car, put the lawnmower back in the barn, locked the door, jumped in the car, drove back to town and just happened to find a parking place right in front of the start of the race. Must have been a guardian angel. Best luck I ever had findin' a parking place in my life!"

I couldn't believe my ears. "Dad, you did all that in the fifteen minutes you were gone, between race number one and race number two?"

"Yup."

I just shook my head.

"Why? Why did you do all that in this heat? You had a heart attack ten years ago, remember? And how did you know you wouldn't miss all the rest of the races when you took off for home like that?"

He smiled. "Well, I just couldn't let the boys down. They worked so hard to win that first race, I couldn't let those old rotten wheels ruin their chances for the rest of the heats. Besides, there was a problem and it just needed to be fixed—that's all."

Well, one thing's for sure. On that hot afternoon in June in the heart of Middle America, my father gave a whole new meaning to the term "Race to the outhouse." He not only saved the day for his nephews and great-niece, he also taught me a valuable lesson: No matter how grave or impossible a situation seems, just bulldoze ahead. Stop procrastinating. Do something. Go somewhere. Fix it. Don't hesitate. Just do it.

Who knows, you just might end up with a two-foot-tall trophy with a shiny little outhouse on top with the door wide open, welcoming you inside.

Don't you just love America?

Life's Too Short to Work Every Day

I PICKED THE BOOK OFF THE SHELF . . . one of those small gift books with a beautiful floral print cover. Inside there were little stories written by grandmothers who shared the reasons they have grandmother names like Cuckoo Nana, Gong Gong, Mu Mu, Hazelnut, Mammy, Mama Bear, Bon Bon, Jo Mama, Chuck, GeeTee, Bylo, Boo-Boo and Mopsy. I have to admit that after the first twenty pages or so I was asking myself, *How many Grandma names are there for goodness sake? And why are so many of them such silly names? Why can't we just be Grandma?*

As I stood there paging through the book, I thought about my six (soon to be seven) grandchildren, Hailey, Hannah, Zachary, Casey, Riley and Chloe, ages eleven, eight, six, five, four and two. They simply call me Grandma Pat or Gramma, and quite frankly I don't care what my grandchildren call me . . . as long as they call me.

After I put that grandmother book down, I began to wonder if I even knew *how* to be a good grandmother. I certainly don't wear cotton flowered dresses and big full-size aprons and bake molasses cookies every week as my Grandma Kobbeman did. I don't sit on a porch swing and rock the evenings away or watch soap operas as my Grandmother Knapp did.

In 1995, when I turned fifty, I water skied behind my brother's boat in Kentucky. That same summer I kayaked in the Pacific Ocean off the coast of Hawaii. In 1997, I rode every scary roller coaster ride at Disneyland. I also bought new in-line skates that summer and plan to be using them for at least twenty years. In 1999, I flew across the Arizona desert in a hot air balloon. In 2000, I rode down a steep alpine slide in Austria. And in 2001, I snorkeled for hours and hours by myself in the Caribbean Sea. You know, typical grandparent adventures.

I thought about my friends who are grandparents. We're certainly different from our grandparents. We have full-time careers. We run corporations and marathons. We belong to clubs, watch the stock market, eat out a lot, exercise regularly and still have time to do the Macarena.

Since all my grandchildren live out of town, I don't see them on a regular basis. In fact, since their parents all have busy careers and whirly-gig lives as I do, I'm lucky if I get to see my grandkids once every month or two.

I'll never forget when Hailey came to my house for her very first "all alone" visit when she was four. She would be alone with me Saturday night, all day Sunday, all day Monday and half of Tuesday before her mother arrived to take her back home. Saturday night and Sunday were a breeze. Hailey, her favorite blankie, latest Beanie Baby and I snuggled together in my big bed. We slept just fine until Hailey sat up in the middle of the night and whispered, "Gramma, you were snoring."

All day Sunday we kept busy with my daughter-in-law and other granddaughter, who were visiting for the day. But on Monday morning when Hailey and I woke up and she assured me that I didn't snore at all that night, I began to fret. *I have books to read and review, an article to write, and a book proposal to get out. I need to be in my office! How am I ever going to get it all done if I have to entertain Hailey all day?*

I'll worry about it later, I thought. For at that moment there were little-girl hugs to be had, waffles to pop in the toaster and birds to feed on the deck with my four-year-old helper.

And so we hugged and rocked and ate, and I held the bird feeder while Hailey scooped up six big cupfuls of tiny seed into the feeder and only half a cup or so landed on the floor.

As we sat in the glider swing on the deck watching the squirrels eat the bird feed, I began to worry again. *I have a column deadline and a talk to prepare.* And yet I wanted so much to be with Hailey. After all, we only had a day and a half left before her mother came. But my work. I needed to work. Or did I?

"Grammie, can we put up the hammock? Remember last summer when we watched the squirrels from the hammock? We could take a nap in it!"

"Let's go to the shed and find that hammock," I said gleefully. We hung the chains into the hooks in the big trees in the backyard and hopped aboard. As we watched a yellow finch and two cardinals flit around the branches high above us while we lay on our backs in that big double-wide hammock, I knew for certain that I was taking the next day and a half off work. Completely.

Hailey and I drew huge pictures on the driveway, using up a whole bucketful of sidewalk chalk. Then she wanted to climb up into her Uncle Andrew's old tree house. She swept all the leaves off the tree house floor and only about half of them landed on my head. We took a long bike ride on the path near my house. Actually I walked while Hailey rode her tiny two-wheeler with the training wheels.

"Grammie, can we go down by the creek?" she squealed when she saw the water.

"Sure! Maybe we'll catch a frog!"

Later that morning we jumped in the car, went shopping for shoes and found just the perfect pair for my wide-footed grandchild. Then we headed to the Playland at McDonalds for lunch. Later that afternoon we ate Combos and candy at the $1.99 movie as we giggled at the funny songs in "Cats Don't Dance."

"Grammie, what are the rules at your house?"

"Rules? I guess I don't have any rules."

"Are you sure there aren't any rules at your house?"

"I'm sure."

"No bedtime?"

"Nope."

"I can stay up until you go to bed?"

"Yup."

"Until late?"

"Sure. We can sleep late tomorrow. You just sit here in my lap so we can snuggle, and I'll read you a couple of books."

"I love you, Grammie."

And so that's how I learned the true meaning of the words I have laminated on top of my computer in my home office:

WRITE THINGS WORTH READING
OR DO THINGS WORTH WRITING.

I learned that doing things like spending an entire day and a half playing with a granddaughter is infinitely more important than sticking to a work routine and getting things done in the office. I learned that grandparents today need to abandon their schedules, meetings, clubs, activities, workload and appointments, and sometimes spend hours at a time drawing silly animals on the driveway or staring at the leaves from a hammock with a four-year-old's head snuggled in the crook of your arm.

Chapter Eight

The Daily Grind and Other Dances

No matter how well we plan our lives, something always happens to put a little splinter in the woodwork. If we're parents, we are responsible for the happiness, education and well-being of our children, and that brings lots of adventures into our lives—some we like, some we don't. No matter how well we plan our lives, we can never keep up with God's grand scheme for how things will actually turn out. Sometimes that white picket fence comes tumbling down, and we find ourselves alone and lonely. Sometimes we lash out, complain, fight, whine and become pesky creatures with the intestinal fortitude of an ant. I know, I've been there.

But along with plowing through the daily grind, if we just keep our goals and hopes and dreams in mind, we'll end up at that place filled with contentment and, more often than not, pure joy. I think it comes from doing the job well and embracing our responsibilities with guts and gusto.

Life's Too Short to Give Up

TO BE PERFECTLY HONEST, the first month was blissful. When Jeanne, age six, Julia, four and Michael, three, and I moved from Missouri to my hometown in northern Illinois the very day of my divorce from their father, I was just happy to find a place where there was no fighting or abuse.

But after the first month I started missing my old friends and neighbors. I missed our lovely, modern, ranch-style brick home in the suburbs of St. Louis, especially after we'd settled into the ninety-eight-year-old white frame house we'd rented, which was all my "post-divorce" income could afford.

In St. Louis we'd had all the comforts: a washer, dryer, dishwasher, TV and car. Now we had none of these. After the first month in our new home, it seemed that we'd gone from middle-class comfort to poverty-level panic.

The bedrooms upstairs in our ancient frame house weren't heated, but somehow the children didn't seem to notice. The linoleum floors, cold on their little feet, simply encouraged them to dress faster in the mornings and to hop into bed quicker in the evenings.

I complained about the cold as the December wind whistled under every window and door in that old frame house. But they giggled about the "funny air places" and simply snuggled under the heavy quilts Aunt Bernadine had brought over the day we moved in.

I was frantic without a TV. "What will we do in the evenings without our favorite shows?" I asked. I felt cheated that the children would miss out on all the Christmas specials. But the children were more optimistic and much more creative than I. They pulled out their games and begged me to play Candyland and Old Maid with them.

We cuddled together on the gray tattered couch the landlord provided and read picture book after picture book from the public library. At their insistence we played records, sang songs, popped popcorn, created magnificent Tinkertoy towers, and played hide-and-seek in our rambling old house. The children taught me how to have fun without a TV.

One shivering December day, just a week before Christmas, after walking the two miles home from my temporary part-time job at a catalog store, I remembered that the week's laundry had to be done that evening. I was dead tired from lifting and sorting other people's Christmas presents, and somewhat bitter, knowing that I could barely afford any gifts for my own children.

As soon as I picked up the kids at the babysitter's, I piled four large laundry baskets full of dirty clothes into their little red wagon, and the four of us headed toward the Laundromat three blocks away.

Inside we had to wait for washing machines and then

for people to vacate the folding tables. The sorting, washing, drying and folding took longer than usual.

Jeanne asked, "Did you bring any raisins or crackers, Mommy?"

"No!" I snapped. "We'll have supper as soon as we get home."

Michael's nose was pressed against the steamy glass window. "Look, Mommy! It's snowing! Big flakes!"

Julia added, "The street's all wet. It's snowing in the air but not on the ground!"

Their excitement only upset me more. If the cold wasn't bad enough, now we had snow and slush to contend with. I hadn't even unpacked the box with their boots and mittens yet.

At last the clean, folded laundry was stacked into the laundry baskets and placed two-baskets deep in the little red wagon. It was pitch dark outside. Six thirty already? No wonder they were hungry! We usually ate at five.

The children and I inched our way into the cold winter evening and slipped along the slushy sidewalk. Our procession of three little people, a crabby mother and four baskets of fresh laundry in an old red wagon moved slowly as the frigid wind bit into our faces. We crossed the busy four-lane street at the crosswalk. When we reached the curb, the front wagon wheels slipped on the ice and tipped the wagon over on its side, spilling all the laundry into a slushy black puddle.

"Oh no!" I wailed. "Grab the baskets, Jeanne! Julia, hold the wagon! Get back up on the sidewalk, Michael!"

I slammed the dirty, wet clothes back into the baskets.

"I hate this!" I screamed. Angry tears spilled out of my eyes.

I hated being poor with no car and no washer or dryer. I hated the weather. I hated being the only parent responsible for three small children. And if you want to know the truth, I hated the whole blasted Christmas season.

When we reached home, I unlocked the door, threw my purse across the room and stomped off to my bedroom for a good cry. I sobbed loud enough for the children to hear. Selfishly, I wanted them to know how miserable I was. Life couldn't get any worse. The laundry was still dirty, we were all hungry and tired, there was no supper started and no outlook for a brighter future.

When the tears finally stopped, I sat up and stared at a wooden plaque of Jesus that was hanging on the wall at the foot of my bed. I'd had that plaque since I was a small child and carried it with me to every house I'd ever lived in. It showed Jesus with His arms outstretched over the earth. Obviously solving the problems of the world.

I kept looking at His face, expecting a miracle. I looked and waited and finally said aloud, "God, can't You do *something* to make my life better?" I desperately wanted an angel on a cloud to come down and rescue me.

Nobody came ... except Julia, who peeked into my bedroom and told me in her tiniest four-year-old voice that she had set the table for supper.

I could hear six-year-old Jeanne in the living room sorting the laundry into two piles, "really dirty, sorta clean, really dirty, sorta clean ..."

Three-year-old Michael popped into my room and gave me a picture of the first snow that he had just colored.

And you know what? At that very moment I *did* see, not one, but *three* angels before me! Three little cherubs, eternally optimistic and, once again, pulling me from gloom and doom into the world of "things will be better tomorrow, Mommy."

Christmas that year was magical as we surrounded ourselves with a very special kind of love, based on the joy of doing simple things together. One thing's for sure: Single parenthood was never again as frightening or as depressing for me as it was the night the laundry fell out of the little red wagon. Those three angels have kept my spirits buoyed and today, more than twenty-five years later, they continue to fill my heart with the presence of God.

Life's Too Short
to Try to Understand Men

SOME PEOPLE THINK I either don't understand men or I'm not that comfortable around them. After all, I've been married, divorced and annulled twice, and one might think that I don't have a clue about men. Perhaps they're right.

The truth of the matter is that although I've been single since 1985 I truly enjoy being around men. And for a single woman, I do have a lot of male friends. Old ones, young ones, middle-agers. Unfortunately, most of them are happily married, priests or young enough to be my sons.

I like to talk to men about everything from politics to religion, from projects in the garage to jokes they hear at work. From "what's wrong with the sump pump" to "let me tell you how to haggle with a used car salesman." I enjoy talking to men about school work, housework, woodwork, books, movies, landscaping, politics and the state of the union. I like to watch football with men.

I like men a lot, but quite simply, I don't understand them. For instance, let's take one simple little autumn activity. Getting rid of leaves. Here's how I do it: I turn on my mulcher mower, mow the yard and pulverize the leaves into smithereens, providing natural fertilizer for the grass. Then I return the mower to the garage and enjoy a good book.

I've observed many men, including my dad, brother, brother-in-law, uncles, cousins, neighbors and friends, in their annual effort to get rid of leaves. Here is a condensed version of how the men I know complete the project: First they buy a full-sized John Deere tractor with an eight-foot blade for grass cutting only. Then they buy a rider mower for tight spaces and a regular lawn mower for really tight spaces. Then they fabricate a huge round leaf blower that also sucks up leaves and attach it to the rider mower. Their next purchase is a wagon to pull behind the rider mower to catch the leaves from the blower. They drive around the yard on the rider mower sucking up leaves and blowing them into the huge wagon.

Next they dump the leaves in the corner of the yard and bag them into huge plastic bags, after which they distribute them to various trees and shrubs for mulch. When a giant wind blows them all over the yard again, they repeat the four previous steps. Then they climb on their full-sized John Deere tractor after attaching a new front-end loader so they can lift the bags of leaves to another part of the yard, behind the shed, so the neighbors can't see them. Then, using the front-end loader, they bring the bags of leaves to the garage area where a new fifteen-hundred-dollar stick-and-leaf mulcher machine now resides . . . a machine that puts out eighty-five thousand decibels of noise with each operation. They take the leaves out of the bags and carefully dump them into the new fifteen-hundred-dollar stick-and-leaf mulcher contraption. Finally they take the mulched-up leaves and dump them into the new spreader attached to the full-sized John Deere tractor and distribute them evenly around the yard to provide natural fertilizer.

It's a man thing. And I suppose you have to love a guy who will go to all that trouble. Think of the exercise he's getting. Communing with nature. Solving one little problem after another. Beats a couch potato with a bag of Ruffles under each arm.

Yes, there's a big difference in the way men and women do things, think, react, solve problems, tackle projects and communicate. Sometimes the difference is unbelievable (see leaf-removal example), and sometimes it's downright exasperating. But most of the time the difference is marvelous.

Men, vive la différence!

Life's Too Short
to Never Say, "I'm Sorry"

IN THE SPRING OF 2001, I got to help some dear friends move from their condo in Florida to a bigger home with three bedrooms and an attached in-ground pool. The day after the move, they left me to house-sit for eight days while they headed for a long-planned skiing vacation in Montana.

I was in heaven. The whole house to myself. A beautiful pool. A bicycle. A lovely neighborhood near the Gulf Intercoastal Waterway and less than a mile to the Gulf of Mexico. Shirley even said I could drive her brand-new PT Cruiser if I wanted to. All week I read, wrote, swam, biked, shopped and relaxed to the max.

One morning I set out on the bike, being very careful on the mile-long stretch of busy road that had no sidewalks or even much of a shoulder for that matter. When I arrived at my shopping destination, I got off the bike and walked it carefully through a busy five-lane intersection. I admit I got into the intersection just as the walk signal changed and it took me longer than normal to maneuver the heavy bike with my big bag and water bottle in the deep metal basket.

All of a sudden, *wham!* I was knocked to the ground

by a car . . . a woman making a left turn ran right into me. I fell on top of the bike, the basket came unhinged, spilling all my stuff into the street. Dazed, I tried to scramble up but fell back down on the bike, terrorized that the maze of traffic would run over me. Finally I was able to stand up. My left leg and right ankle hurt like crazy, but I managed to gather the bike, bag and basket, and hobble out of the intersection.

I dropped the bike on the grass next to the sidewalk to try to reattach the basket. I couldn't figure it out. Suddenly, I just stood there and the tears came. No one had stopped to help me. Even the woman who'd knocked me down had gone on. I didn't know a soul for miles, didn't know if I was really hurt or just in shock, and knew I couldn't ride home two miles carrying that big heavy bike basket under my arm.

I had never felt more isolated in my entire life. As cars whizzed by I stood there, alone, scraped, bruised, confused and scared. Just then I looked up and saw a woman across the street standing next to her car, waving her arms like a wild woman. When she got my attention, she motioned for me to meet her in the grocery store parking lot just a few feet from where I was standing. I nodded and gingerly inched my way to the blacktop.

"Oh, my dear, my dear, are you okay? I'm so sorry! It was my fault. I didn't even look to the right. All I saw was that green arrow and I gunned it to make that left turn. Are you hurt? I have insurance. Do you need to go to the hospital?" She couldn't seem to stop talking to hear my answers.

"No, I don't think I'm hurt. Just a few bruises and scrapes. My ankle hurts a bit, but I don't think it's serious."

At that moment the tears almost started up again and I could hardly talk.

"Are you sure you're okay? I'm so sorry. If the bike is damaged I'll buy a new one. Honestly, I don't know what to say."

"Well," I stammered, "will you write down your name and phone number just in case?"

"Oh yes, here, I have paper and pen in the car. My name's Beverly."

"It's just that I'm house-sitting for some friends who went to Montana and I don't know anyone around here. And all I can say is that I was really, really sad that no one stopped to help me when I ended up flat down in the intersection. At least you stopped. I feel a lot better now. I thought it was a hit-and-run."

"Oh goodness, no. I just didn't look before I turned. I am *so sorry*. Where are you from, my dear?"

"Wisconsin," I said quietly.

"Why, I'm from Wisconsin, too! What town do you live in?"

"Milwaukee. Oak Creek, actually."

"Honey, I was born and raised in Milwaukee and lived there all my life until twenty years ago when we moved down here."

I nodded at Beverly. "My friends Wally and Shirley just moved into a new house over by St. Jerome's Church on Hamlin. That's their parish. They're in the choir there."

"Would you believe that I'm the church housekeeper at St. Jerome's?"

Well, needless to say, Beverly and I were old chums by the time we parted. I figured out how to get the basket back on the bike, rode home, and within the week my bruises and scrapes were healed.

But most importantly, my feelings were healed, too. It's amazing how powerful those two little words are. Two little words from Beverly's mouth to my ears made all the difference between an adventure and a highly stressful tragedy.

Two little words. *I'm sorry*. And she meant it.

Life's Too Short
to Hate Piano Recitals

ONE OF THE THINGS MENTIONED on the back of the parenthood card that we all carry in our wallets (yeah, right!) is the list of activities we parents must attend with our children. Here is a partial list: band, choir and orchestra concerts, ball games, dance recitals, music contests, art shows, science projects, Boy, Girl and Cub Scout meetings/dinners and Pinewood Derbies, swim meets, cheerleading practice, school plays, open house, parent/teacher conferences, award ceremonies and piano recitals. Remember, this was just a partial list.

During my nearly thirty years of full-time parenting, I attended enough child-centered events to practically guarantee me a very high place in heaven. Once, while I sat in the audience waiting for what seemed like forever for the room to fill up with eager parents, grandparents and friends of the performers so I could watch my daughter Jeanne's umpteenth piano recital to begin, I looked around and took notes. Here is what I wrote on that Sunday afternoon many years ago:

Look at that poor girl. All pink and ruffly. Bet her mother picked out that dress. She looks like she's about to die of embarrassment. The blue jeans skirt and sailor top would have been much better. Ruffles, indeed. And black patent leather heels? At her age? She must be ten or eleven. A mother ought to know better.

Has it been a whole year since the last one? Another year gone already. It's too hot in here. And these chairs! Metal folding chairs squeaking and creaking as we all shift haunches. This particular church hall has a definite acoustical problem. What else is new? All church halls have acoustical problems. Why doesn't someone open a window?

Love these lights. Six four-foot-long fluorescent bulbs stretched end to end clear across the room. And six more lights back there. Charming. Why couldn't this have been in the church with candlelight instead of naked fluorescents? In church, all these up-and-coming Van Cliburns would be sitting still for fear of breaking the spell of that holy place. Instead, we get twenty fidgeters in the first two rows yapping away.

Wish that kid would stop tugging at his sports coat like that. So what if it feels like a strait jacket and his mother should have handed it down to his little brother already. Piano recital is the only time all year he has to wear a suit. Might as well make it last through one more ordeal. Love those white socks he's wearing under the too-short pants.

At last. Mrs. Mighty Eighty-Eight-Keys-on-the-Keyboard appears, smiling, gloating over her twenty charges as if they were prize peonies at the state fair.

It begins. The annual keyboard assault. The first kid is someone named Heather. Naturally. Heathers are supposed to play piano. Heather gives it the old hunt and peck touch.

"Tick Tock Musical Clock" doesn't quite have them jumping in the aisles, but at least the kid got up there, did her thing and didn't cry.

Next we have Angela, Amy, Jennifer, Brenda. Where are the boys? Don't boys like piano?

What time is it? It's five down and fifteen to go, and the temperature in here is going ballistic. I don't think I'm going to live through this. My fanny is totally asleep. There must be permanent damage to my backside. It's not good to sit on hard, cold chairs for this long. I know, because of the Preparation H commercials on TV. How can the bottom side of me be so cold and the rest of me be so hot? At least they're going to have refreshments after this. Brownies, maybe. *Mmm*. Haven't had a good, chewy brownie for months. Don't suppose they'd have champagne punch. No, not in a church hall.

Darin, David, Wendy, Michael, Opal. Opal? My great-great aunt's name was Opal, for heaven's sake. Don't tell me that name is coming back. Well, at least we have some boys in the program.

How can Mrs. Mighty Eighty-Eight's husband stand to listen to this day after day in their home? Maybe he wears earplugs. How can he concentrate on the latest cops and robbers show on TV? How does he get through *60 Minutes*? He must be a schoolteacher and is used to such things from wee people.

"Spinning Song." Played that a thousand times myself. I still can't walk by a piano without tossing out a few measures of "Spinning Song."

"Cowboy Boogie." Never made the top ten, but Rodney sure is enjoying it. Somebody should tell Rodney that a boogie doesn't have a beat like that.

"Sunrise, Sunset." Ah, my favorite from Fiddler on the Roof. Used to be my favorite, until today. *Whoa!* What's she doing to this beautiful piece? Slow down, sweetie! Sunrise, sunset. You know, the old guy is reflecting on the beginning and the end of his life. It's a slow, romantic, questioning kind of song. This kid has the guy going up and down and in and out to the beat of an REO Speedwagon rocker! I can't take this! My favorite song mutilated by the impatient fingers of a prepubescent sixth-grader who's probably more concerned about the fact that she's wearing a bra for the first time.

How many more to go? Eight? What would happen if I fainted? Would they rush me out in an ambulance, take me to a nice air-conditioned hospital and bring me a chocolate milkshake to perk me up? I could just leave and go to the restroom. That might kill two or three performances. Maybe the ladies in the back need help with the cookies. I could pour punch. Fold napkins. Count the guests. Guard the brownies. But, no, I have to sit here and listen and fidget.

Look at those goofy parents. The kid plays "Sandbox Blues" with three fingers and his folks are up there in front of everybody taking flash pictures during the entire forty-two second performance. Wouldn't a picture with the kid sitting at the piano after the recital, pretending to be playing, be just as effective? I mean, who cares whether the picture in the photo album was taken during the exact moment Johnny was trembling his way through "Blue Birds and Field Mice"?

Well, finally. My daughter. Oh, she's smiling. And standing up straight! Look at that girl. Beautiful, just beautiful. *Ah* . . . the fingers fly. At last, something with meat in it. A piano piece worth listening to. Is it my imagination or are people sitting up straighter, trying to get a closer look at that child genius who is filling the room with such marvelous sounds?

My face is flushing. My heart is going to burst. "Sonata Number Five in G Major." Even the title sounds impressive. I grab my camera to take a picture quickly before she's finished. Sure glad I brought the tape recorder. Someday her grandchildren will love hearing this. Someday when she's a famous pianist, NBC will do an interview. They'll come to our home and ask if, by chance, I have any recollections of her earlier piano recitals, before she became a virtuoso. I'll smile demurely, excuse myself, and reach into my drawer of keepsakes and produce the tape. This tape. The tape of this smiling, beautiful, talented, thirteen-year-old genius playing "Sonata Number Five in G Major" almost by heart. My daughter.

What? She's finished already? What? No standing ovation? Probably because there are still four students left to play. Oh goodness, four more. All classical. Four more, long, boring, mistake-riddled pieces, no doubt. Four more teeny boppers separated mercilessly from their blue jeans, foisted into "going to your sister's wedding" clothes and forced to send the audience miles away in irreverent day-dream reveries.

Ack. So the kid is playing "Claire de Lune." So what if it's perfect. I'm sure my daughter could do better. Besides, this kid has probably been taking piano lessons three years longer than my daughter.

Finally. The last one. "Prelude in C-Sharp Minor" by Rachmaninoff. Sounds impressive, but that's probably the only thing the kid can play. They should hear my daughter at home. What a repertoire.

Piano recital. At least it gives me a chance to gloat over what a genius I've produced. Now she's shoving cookies and punch into that lovely face. Asks if she can go home with Lisa to work on their parts in the school play.

I walk out alone and a little lonely. But deep inside I smile because I know that the money spent on piano lessons is well worth it and that someday my daughter will thank me for my support.

Next night: Pinewood Derby, 6:00 PM. High-school band concert 8:00 PM, Tuesday: cheerleading tryouts. Dress rehearsal for the school play. Oh boy!

Life's Too Short
to Lie about Anything

MY HUSBAND was a high-school administrator who always got a kick out of the excuses kids gave for being late to school. One day, four senior boys sauntered in around 11:00 AM instead of the usual 7:45 AM when classes started.

"Mr. Lorenz, we had a flat tire and had trouble getting it changed," the boys chorused.

"Okay, men, follow me," Harold replied. He placed each boy in a different room and then went from room to room telling each one, "Son, I'm going to give you a little test. Don't worry, it's easy. Just one question. Simply write down on this piece of paper which tire was flat."

When Harold collected the four papers he learned that the front right, back left and back right tires had all been flat. Each of the boys served time in detention for one week without so much as a complaint.

Fact: When you lie, you *will* get caught.

Who are the people who lie? Shel Silverstein says it best in his poem "Invitation."

> If you are a dreamer, come in,
> If you are a dreamer, a wisher, a liar,
> A hope-er, a pray-er, a magic bean buyer . . .
> If you're a pretender, come sit by my fire

For we have some flax-golden tales to spin.

Come in!

Come in!

On her way to school, six-year-old Annie picked three beautiful snowball-sized yellow flowers and wrapped them carefully in a wet paper towel she'd brought from the kitchen. Trouble is she picked them out of Mrs. Eberly's prized flower garden without permission.

"Annie, Mrs. Eberly called today and said you picked three of her prized mums."

"No, I didn't. Honest, Mama."

"Annie, she saw you from her kitchen window."

"It was somebody else. Honest, Mama."

"Annie, the deed is done. Now we have to figure out why you did it and how you can repay Mrs. Eberly."

Big tears welled up in Annie's eyes.

"I wanted them for my teacher. She's going to have a baby."

"It still wasn't right to take someone else's flowers. What do you think you should do?"

"Mama, please don't make me tell her I'm sorry. She won't like me ever again!"

"Mrs. Eberly is upset. She feels badly that you didn't ask her permission to pick her flowers. Annie, I think she'll like you very much if you tell her you're sorry, and I'm sure she'll forgive you as well. How can you make up for the missing flowers?"

"I could buy her some new ones with the money I got for my birthday."

"Great idea, honey. I saw some beautiful potted mums at the florist yesterday."

Fact: When you lie, it is imperative to ask for forgiveness. Trust is too precious a gift to lose forever.

Lying, unfortunately, is a common thing. Both children and adults lie for a number of different reasons. To protect themselves from ridicule. To cover up a wrongful deed. To avoid doing work. To make themselves look good in the eyes of a parent, child or friend. Or to cover up some sort of dysfunction within the family, friend or work structure.

"My husband couldn't come to the parent-teacher conferences because he had an important business meeting."

Deadbeat hubby may have been home drunk on the sofa, as usual. But the wife doesn't want the outside world to know anything's wrong in her world. Facing the problem or asking for help or insisting the spouse get help is just too painful or difficult, so she lies to cover up.

Jody, age seventeen, told her parents that she and a friend were going to play tennis at a nearby tennis court. She got permission to use the family car to pick up her friend. But instead of playing tennis, Jody crammed six teens into the car and they spent the evening cruising from one suburb to another. Driving the family car without a specific destination in mind was not allowed by Jody's parents. Cruising aimlessly, looking for friends or a party, playing the radio loudly, honking and waving at people, and being distracted by her friends in the car for hours on end could have resulted in a tragic accident.

Jody's lie to her parents served a purpose, for her at

least. Lying among teenagers is often used to defeat parents, escape punishment, seek revenge or generate excitement. Obviously, Jody was interested in the excitement of cruising in her parents' car without their approval. Unfortunately, her lie could have caused a serious accident or injury because of her lack of driving experience.

Psychologists say the goal for parents or spouses is to create an atmosphere in which there is no need to lie. Children should be given a certain amount of freedom, trust and confidence. Mistrusting, playing detective and overreacting will often result in a child who lies more frequently and whose lies become more and more involved. Therefore, if a parent discovers that a child is lying, the most important thing to do is examine the relationship between parent and child and work to open up channels of communication. A family meeting may be in order. Or take a walk or a drive with the child so you have a captive audience and you can both share your viewpoints without interruptions.

If you or someone you know is in the habit of lying, there are a number of things you can do to help. First of all, don't expect anyone to be perfect. If we feel we can't possibly live up to the expectations of others, we may start lying just so we won't disappoint them. Try to eliminate some of the stress in the person's life who is lying. Are they involved in too many regulated after-school and weekend activities? Is the adult working too hard, too many hours or has too many other responsibilities? Eliminating stress, working less, playing and relaxing more often eliminate the need for lying. Keeping the lines of communication open helps tremendously. Make time each day to talk to each family member one-on-one, no matter how busy you are. People who lie often just don't have the time to communicate properly, and a fast lie serves their hectic, harried, stressful purpose. Defuse that by pushing the pause button on life every once in a while and slowing down.

If you or someone you know has become a liar, pretender, spinner of tales or a magic bean buyer, today is the day for a reality check. Trust is too precious to waste, and life is too short to lie your way through it. The truth shall, indeed, set you free. The whole truth and nothing but.

Life's Too Short
Not to Have a Chore List

GOODNESS KNOWS I would never qualify as a marriage counselor, but because I've been without a husband since 1985 I think I'm at least good at observing other people's marriages and figuring out what makes them work so beautifully.

My dear friends Wally and Shirley retired to Florida from Wisconsin in 1992. In 2001, they sold their two-bedroom Florida condominium and bought a house with three bedrooms and an attached in-ground swimming pool. Wally's in his seventies and Shirley's not far behind, and instead of making their lives easier, simpler and smaller, they're expanding.

Shortly after I arrived in Florida, we three worked for four days straight packing boxes, hauling boxes, unpacking boxes. Wally made long lists every day of things he had to do at the new house. Fix the door locks, put the garage shelves together, learn how to care for the pool, fix this, change that, unpack the seventy boxes in the garage.

Shirley and I kept busy lining the shelves in the kitchen, pantry and bathrooms, then unloaded at least a hundred boxes and found places for everything. We sorted, piled, swept, decorated, arranged, rearranged and laughed our way through the move.

Tensions mounted a few times between husband and wife, as they always do during the most stressful times in our lives. Moving is right up there with death of a spouse, loss of a job, disease and divorce.

By the time the move was complete, and Wally, Shirley and I were cavorting in their new pool, I'd learned a lot about what makes a good marriage tick. Even when one spouse flares up and yells a bit during the most hectic times, the important part of the good marriage equation is that both partners get over the little snit quickly. Wally and Shirley can snap at each other, and it's over and done with. Two minutes later they're back to normal, joking and going about the business of life.

The key is knowing that it's almost always stress and bottled up frustration over other things, not the spouse, that cause someone to blow. It's okay to blow. Just don't take it personally, and try hard to laugh about something as soon after the blowing as possible. Chances are the whole incident will be forgotten in less time than it takes to tear down a cardboard box after it's unpacked.

Another thing I learned about marriage from Wally and Shirley is the importance of an equitable division of chores, especially after both parties are retired. After all, neither of these retired teachers is out there beating their brains in the real world to make a living, so it stands to reason that all household, yard and mechanical chores should be divided as equally as possible.

Shirley says they had a big sit-down powwow one evening and together they made two lists of work to be done on a regular basis for each of them. Shirley typed the lists and taped them to the inside of the kitchen cabinet. Here they are, in minute, marriage-saving detail . . . Wally and Shirley's lists of weekly chores:

Shirley: grocery shop; fix dinner; make granola bread, cakes, muffins, etc.; vacuum and wash tile floors; dust all furniture; wash and iron clothes; balance checkbook and pay bills; feed cats and clean litter box; make coffee; clean oven and refrigerator; clean and wax bathroom and kitchen sinks and countertops; trim bushes, tend flowers and garden.

Wally: last-minute shopping; fix lunch; vacuum carpets; fold laundry; check bills; empty dishwasher; make bed; clean toilets and shower; fill soap dispensers; maintain auto repair; sweep garage; put out garbage, daily papers and recycle box; pest control; repair outside stuff; wash and wax cars.

As long as both parties agree to their division of chores, it's amazing how well this system works. I love it when I'm visiting and Shirley may be outside trimming bushes while Wally's inside fixing lunch.

The grit, grime, gusto and glory of household chores are very much like marriage itself. To make it work, accept the fact that little snits are bound to happen. Just get over them in less time than it takes to slam a door. No pouting allowed. Take a deep breath and crack a joke. Works every time. Also, talk about what each of you expects from the other. Write down the things each of you will be responsible for and then do your chores without prompting from the other.

Time to go. I think Wally has lunch ready.

Chapter Nine

Healthy, Wealthy and Wise

The older we get, the more we appreciate good health as the true standard for a happy life. It's a simple formula really. Take care of yourself and chances are you'll be healthier and therefore happier.

But sometimes it doesn't work that way. Sometimes a curve ball hits us smack in the head. That's where strong faith comes into play. No matter what happens to us, if we have faith as tiny as a mustard seed, we can move mountains with God's help. That's what makes this life so doggone grand and positively mind-boggling. We humans are capable of such incredible things no matter how much bad stuff happens to us. We are grand champion rebounders!

If you ever get a tad bit discouraged, just remember, we only need five things to be happy: someone to love, something to do, something to hope for, faith and laughter. If you have all these things in your life you are blessed indeed because you are already healthy, wealthy and wise.

Life's Too Short to Drink Syrup

WHEN I FIRST HEARD the words "Four Hour Fasting Glucose Tolerance Test," the word *fasting* made my brain quiver and my body weak. How long did they expect me to fast, for crying out loud, without crying out loud?

On test morning, without my usual hefty breakfast under my belt, I checked in at the hospital as an outpatient. A white-coated technician put a tourniquet around my upper arm and jumped back in amazement at the size of the bulging blue vein in the crook of my arm. One thing I have is good veins, standing high, dark and proud, just waiting for a slick needle to sap their juices.

Next, the pièce de résistance. At first I thought it was my reward for having great veins. The lab technician produced a bottle of what looked like orange soda pop. I figured, *Hey, this isn't going to be so bad*. Since I missed my orange juice earlier, this would be a nice substitute.

The pop bottle liquid was ice cold and tasted like carbonated orange Kool Aid made with four cups of sugar instead of one. The first four ounces went down without a hitch. The next four ounces I forced, telling myself that this was better than nothing in my poor, empty, breakfastless stomach. The third four ounces I swallowed in sips.

My stomach was telling me to knock it off. The last four ounces refused to move past my lips. Then the smiling technician reminded me that I had to down it all within the next two minutes or else. I'm a lover, not a fighter, so I took a deep breath and swallowed hard.

At least part one was over. "Don't leave the hospital during the rest of the test and don't exert yourself." What did they expect, cartwheels and sprints in the hallway? It was all I could do to keep the last four ounces of the liquid sugar in my stomach.

Then the lab folks gave me a little schedule card with the times they'd need urine and blood samples. Five more times each, at half-hour then one-hour intervals.

8:30 AM. The effects of the orange nectar were starting to claw at the deep recesses of my stomach. I wondered if I was going to be sick. I bit my tongue and stared at a torn piece of wallpaper in the hallway for five minutes until the crisis was over.

8:45 AM. Another donation into the great urine bank. As much of that stuff as the human race produces every day you'd think there'd be a use for it. Couldn't medical labs turn it into an energy-efficient fuel? People could drink lots more water and donate the by-product in gallon containers.

With the onset of those thoughts, I knew my mind was going. Well, what did they expect, starving me like this?

Another blood extraction. At five to seven milliliters a crack, I figured I'd be completely blood-let by noon. Tried to remember how much blood there is in the human body, but high-school biology failed me. Then I wondered how long it would take to generate new blood. I wanted to get caught up as soon as possible. I like having all my original parts.

Read a few magazines, then saw a nurse friend slip into the snack bar. I caught up with her, joined her at a table, then watched her consume a cup of coffee with cream and sugar, a fresh peach and a sweet roll covered with raisins, walnuts, or maybe they were pecans, lots of icing and cinnamon. She spread a whole pat of real butter on it. Can't remember what we talked about.

Tried to recall the last time I missed breakfast. Having been an honor student in the "Breakfast Is Your Most Important Meal" club, I realized I'd probably never missed breakfast in my entire life.

9:15 AM. Another urine specimen. More blood. Feeling like a living sacrifice. Getting sleepy. Yawning every five minutes or so. But that could be psychological. The more I think about yawning, the more I yawn. Like malted milk balls. The more I eat, the more I eat.

Read an article about Marie Osmond. Every word, eight pages, on the edge of my seat. Now I know this test is affecting my mind. What could possibly be happening to me that would make me spend this much time reading about a gorgeous, rich girl who's five feet, five inches tall and weighs ninety-five pounds?

10:15 AM. More donations. I try to maintain some control over my life by insisting they switch arms each time they puncture my vein. Now the score is tied. Two in the left arm, two in the right. Both arms looking haggard, but not as haggard as I feel.

11:15 AM. Stomach growling. Feeling weak, tired, bored. How many nurses, doctors and sick people can one watch walking down hallways? How long can one watch morning TV without wondering if your brain is mashed potatoes?

11:50 AM. Just read a booklet, "The Electro-Encephalogram. What It Is and How It Works," word for word. Why did I do that? Who cares?

12:00 NOON. Feeling strange. Weepy. Something's definitely out of whack here. I actually shed tears during a rerun of *Love Boat*. Then read an article about why hugging is good for us. Cried twice during that.

12:15 PM and into the final stretch. One more urine specimen and the final blood sample.

"That's it. You can leave now. Be sure you eat something when you get home."

"When I get home? I'm heading for the hospital cafeteria for a double cheeseburger, fries, a side order of scrambled eggs, a couple tacos and a chef salad. Then when I get home, I'll have something to eat!"

Four Hour Fasting Glucose Tolerance Test. I'd survived. The diagnosis wasn't the suspected diabetes, but rather a mild case of hypoglycemia, low blood sugar . . . ten times more common than diabetes.

Well, what did they expect, starving me like that and taking all that blood? No wonder my blood sugar was low.

Oh well, if I hadn't taken the test I never would have known just how hard Marie Osmond has to work to keep her weight down to ninety-five pounds.

Life's Too Short to Smoke

THE PROFESSOR SAID, "Write an informative, personal opinion piece about a controversial issue." My research was complete. I had given the subject a great deal of thought and was ready to type up my final draft. The children, ages thirteen, eleven, ten and three, promised to leave me alone for two hours. I began typing.

Smoking, Slow-Motion Suicide

Why don't they quit? People die from smoking. It's a debilitating habit. It's expensive, dirty and irritating to nonsmokers.

Why don't they quit? The biggest problem is nicotine, an addictive fatal poison, also used commercially as an insecticide.

Mom, I'm starving, I mean positively starving. I mean really, I might die. Okay if I have a peanut butter sandwich, milk and an apple? What's for supper? Liver and onions? You must be joking! So maybe I should have two peanut butter sandwiches. Why not? Oh, gross. How anyone on this earth can eat liver and live to tell about it is beyond me. I mean really. It gags me, Mom. Maybe if I drown it in ketchup I could force it down. That is if I don't die first from the fumes.

When smokers try to give up tobacco, withdrawal from nicotine creates anxiety, which in turn results in acidic urine. This flushes nicotine faster than usual through the body and triggers the physical need to light up another cigarette so that the amount of nicotine in the body gets back up to the usual level of addiction. A few moments after the first drag, nicotine reaches the brain, but within twenty to thirty minutes it has dissipated to other organs. Another fix is needed to counter the change in brain wave activity. That's why the time lag for heavy smokers between cigarettes is precisely twenty to thirty minutes.

Mom, I got a hundred on my times tables test today even though there were eighty problems and we had to do them in a minute and a half and I did them all in one minute and Mr. Bolzman said I was the first person to get a hundred on the first try in about six years so he gave me eighty dollars, you know, those play dollars so we can bid on stuff at the end of the year, well, anyway, now I have fourteen thousand dollars in my account and he said I can still take the test every day with the other kids until they all get one hundred and every time I get a hundred I get eighty more dollars.

The main reason people don't quit smoking is that they don't have the courage to fight through withdrawal from the drug nicotine.

Hi, Mom! Hate to bother you, but David wants to know if I can go to the jumps with him. I fixed the handlebars on my bike, well me and David did, so anyway now we're going to the jumps and try out suicide run. It's great! About ten feet deep and the hill is like a cliff. Now that my handlebars don't wobble I know I can make it. I already practiced my drum this morning, don't you remember? Oh, sorry, I didn't know you were still sleeping then. So, can I go with David to the jumps? Oh, this guy at school said there was this dirt-bike rally next Sunday that the firemen put on for anybody with a dirt bike. Wow! It'll be so great. We could all go. You know, Dad, you, everybody, and you guys could watch me and every-thing. So can I go to David's now or what?

It's also very difficult for this country's fifty-three mil-lion smokers to go through the psychological trauma of getting the cigarette monkey off their backs.

Mommy, tie my shoe. Can I go to Nicky's house? Michael won't let me play baseball and I want to. Can I have some juice? Michael threw the ball at me! Mommy, can I go to Nicky's house? He came here first, but then he went home, so now can I go to his house? Tie my shoe, Mommy!

Every year more than one million young Americans are seduced into the smoking habit by the more than eight hundred million dollars spent each year on cigarette adver-tising. The ads make smoking look glamorous, sexy and very much a part of the good life.

Mrs. Williams is at the door, Mom. She wants you to watch Jennifer for an hour. I can already smell that liver. If I live through this night it'll be a miracle. I finished practicing my piano and did part of my homework. I have to put some-thing in my stomach to pad it before the liver onslaught. Okay if I have a doughnut? Come on, Mom, that peanut butter sandwich did not hold me. Be a sport. It's at least forty-five minutes till supper, right?

Cigarette smoking kills more than three hundred thousand Americans each year and cripples millions more. Smoking causes heart disease, bronchitis, emphysema and other deadly diseases. The smokers get sick, and the tobacco companies get rich.

Hey, Mom, okay if Wendy spends the night Friday? The only thing on the calendar is the football game and Jeanne has to baby-sit at the Williams' and Grandpa and Grandma might be coming and there's your writers' meeting but that's over at eight-thirty, right, so can't Wendy come? She could ride the bus home with me and Saturday you could take us roller skating. Huh, Mom?

Smoking is not only a health hazard to the smokers themselves, but also to nonsmokers. In fact, nonsmokers may inhale almost as many dangerous and cancer-causing agents as smokers.

Mom! I want to watch the game and the girls are watching some dumb show and it's my day. I already cleaned up the kitchen and my homework's done and it's my day to pick the show. It's the championship! I gotta see that game! Mom, are you listening to me?

What about the rights of nonsmokers? Considering they are in the majority (sixty-eight percent of adult women and fifty-seven percent of adult men do not smoke), it's a sad fact that nonsmokers' rights to clean air are constantly being abused.

Mom! The phone's for Julia, where is she? How long till we eat?

The fifty-three million people in this country who do

smoke are contributing to the pollution, irritation, discomfort and possible disease of those who do not smoke. But the nonsmokers are fighting back. Most public places now have no-smoking signs posted or at least have separate smoking sections. Almost all airlines, theaters and many restaurants arc now smoke-free.

Mommy! I can't find my blankie! My green one. Mommy! I want it now. And a cracker. Where's Daddy? Julia won't play with me. Michael told me I can't watch the game with him. Mom-meeeeeee!

It's important for nonsmokers to remember that they do have rights. If you're a nonsmoker and you object to smoke being blow in your face, speak up!

Mom, Aunt Martha wants to know if you'll take her to play Bingo tonight. Why don't we order pizza instead of having liver? Please, Mom. So can you take Aunt Martha or not? She's on the phone.

The next time someone asks you, "Do you mind if I smoke?" do yourself and the person asking the question a big favor and say, "Yes, I *do* mind."

Hey, Mom, Dad's home. What time is supper? We're all starving up here!

Life's Too Short to Fear Change

IN 1993 I WAS INTO my eighth year as a single parent, had three kids in college, my youngest had just become a teenager, my unmarried daughter had just given birth to my first grandchild, and I was about to break up with a very nice man I'd dated for more than two years. It wasn't the best year of my life, to be sure, and I was spending lots of time feeling sorry for myself.

That April a magazine for which I'd written some stories called and asked me to interview a woman who lived in a small town in Minnesota. So during Easter vacation, Andrew, my thirteen-year-old, and I drove across two states to meet Jan Turner.

Andrew dozed most of the way during the long drive, but every once in a while I'd start a conversation.

"She's handicapped, you know."

"So what's wrong with her? Does she have a disease?"

"No. She had to have both arms and legs amputated."

"Wow. How does she get around?"

"I'm not sure. We'll see when we get there."

"Does she have any kids?"

"Two boys. And she's a single parent, too. Only she's never been married. She adopted her two boys.

The oldest one, Tyler, is about your age. Cody's the younger one."

"So what happened to her?"

"Four years ago Jan was just like me, a busy single mother. She was a full-time music teacher at a grade school. Taught all sorts of musical instruments. She was also the music director at her church. She told me on the phone that she and the boys spent weekends and summers camping, fishing and hiking."

"Must be nice. We *never* go camping, fishing or hiking."

"We hike in the park."

"That's not the same as real hiking."

"Well, I just don't like to hike in the wilderness without another adult."

Andrew fell asleep again before I could finish telling him what little I *did* know about what happened to Jan. As I drove across Minnesota I began to wonder how the woman I was about to meet could cope with such devastating news that all four limbs had to be amputated. *How did she learn to survive? Did she have live-in help?* I wondered.

When we arrived in the small town of Willmar, I called Jan from our hotel to tell her that I could come to her house and pick her and the boys up so they could swim at our hotel while we talked.

"That's okay, Pat, I can drive. The boys and I will be there in ten minutes. Would you like to go out to eat first? There's a restaurant close to your hotel."

"Sure, that'll be fine," I said haltingly, wondering what

it would be like to eat in a public restaurant with a woman who had no arms or legs. *And how on earth does she drive?* I wondered.

Ten minutes later Jan pulled up in front of the hotel in a big, older model car. She got out, walked over to me with perfect posture on legs and feet that looked every bit as real as mine, and extended her right arm with its shiny hook on the end to shake my hand. "Hello, Pat, I'm sure glad to meet you. And this must be Andrew."

I grabbed her hook, pumped it a bit and smiled sheepishly. "*Uh*, yes, this is Andrew." I looked in the backseat of her car and smiled at the two boys, who grinned back. Cody, the younger one, was practically effervescent at the thought of going swimming in the hotel pool after dinner.

Jan bubbled as she slid back behind the driver's seat, "So hop in. Cody, move over and make room for Andrew."

We arrived at the restaurant, went through the cafeteria line, paid for our food, ate and talked amidst the chattering of our three sons. The only thing I had to do for Jan that entire evening was unscrew the lid on the ketchup bottle. As I struggled with the tight lid, I remember feeling dumbfounded that Jan drove a car, carried her own food tray, pulled the dollars and change out of her wallet for the waitress, and fed herself as if she'd been born with those hooks instead of hands.

Later that night, as our three sons splashed in the pool, we sat on the side and talked. Jan told me about life before her illness.

"We were a typical single-parent family. You know,

busy all the time. On weekends we did all those roustabout things young boys like." I winced when she mentioned hiking, camping, fishing and hunting, remembering Andrew's comment in the car. I'd never done *any* of those things with my own sons.

"We have dogs, and we love the outdoors. Life was so good, in fact, that I was seriously thinking about adopting a third child."

Once again my conscience stung. I had to face it. The woman next to me was better at parenting than I ever thought about being.

Jan continued. "One Sunday in November 1989 I was playing my trumpet in front of the church when I suddenly felt weak, dizzy and nauseous. I struggled down the aisle, motioned for the boys to follow me and drove home. I crawled into bed, but by evening I knew I had to get help."

Jan explained that by the time she arrived at the hospital, she was comatose. Her blood pressure had dropped so much that her body was already shutting down.

By the third day, after many tests, the doctors told Jan that she had pneumococcal pneumonia, the same bacterial infection that took the life of Muppets creator Jim Henson. One of its disastrous side effects turns on the body's clotting system and causes the blood vessels to plug up. Because there was no blood flow to her hands or feet, she quickly developed gangrene in all four extremities. Two weeks after being admitted to the hospital, Jan's arms had to be amputated at mid-forearm and her legs at mid-shin.

Just before the surgery she said she cried out, "Oh,

God, no! How can I live without arms and legs, feet or hands? Never walk again? Never play the trumpet, guitar, piano or any of the instruments I teach? I'll never be able to hug my sons or take care of them . . . let alone take care of myself! Oh, God, don't let me be dependent on others for the rest of my life!"

Six weeks after the amputations, as her dangling limbs healed, a doctor talked to Jan about prosthetics. She said Jan could learn to walk, drive a car, go back to school, even go back to teaching.

Jan found that hard to believe, so she picked up her Bible, determined to keep her heart and mind open. The book fell open to Romans, chapter twelve (TLB). Her eyes dropped to verse two: "Don't copy the behavior and customs of this world, but be a new and different person with a fresh newness in all you do and think. Then you will learn from your own experience how his ways will really satisfy you."

Jan thought about that. *Be a new and different person with a fresh newness in all you do.* She decided to give it a try and started to look forward to stepping into her new legs and taking those first steps. Even though the skin on her limbs had healed after surgery, she wasn't prepared for the pain of the one hundred pounds of body weight pushing down into the prosthetics. With a walker strapped onto her forearms near the elbow and a therapist on either side, she could only wobble on her new legs for two to three minutes before she collapsed in exhaustion and pain.

"Take it slowly," Jan recalled saying to herself. "Be a

new person in all that you do and think, but take it one step at a time."

The next day she tried on the prosthetic arms, a crude system of cables, rubber bands and hooks operated by a harness across the shoulders. By moving her shoulder muscles she was able to open and close the hooks to pick up and hold objects, dress and feed herself . . . do almost everything she used to do, only in a new and different way.

Within a few months, Jan learned that being different wasn't so bad after all. For one thing, she had always wished she was taller. So each time she got new prosthetics for her legs, she had them made an inch longer. She went from being five feet five to five feet eight.

Every year since she was a little girl, Jan said her hands and feet would freeze during the bitter cold Minnesota winters. But now? Jan giggled as she rubbed her short brown hair with her left hook. "My hands and feet haven't been cold since 1989! And I'm the only person I know who can take the food out of the oven without hot pads. If I step in a mud puddle by mistake, I don't even notice that cold, wet feeling on my socks and shoes.

"When I finally got to go home after four months of physical and occupational therapy, I was nervous about what life would be like with my boys and me alone in the house. But when I got home, I got out of the car, walked up the steps to our house, hugged my boys with all my might, and we haven't looked back since."

As Jan and I continued to talk, Cody, who'd climbed out of the pool, stood close to his mom with his arm around her shoulders. As she told me about her newly improved cooking skills, Cody grinned, "Yup," he said, "she's a better mom now than before she got sick, because now she can even flip pancakes!"

The next day, Andrew and I visited Jan and her sons at their home where she demonstrated how she puts on and takes off her arms and legs each morning and evening. She showed me how she washes her hair, using a washcloth with shampoo on it to rub onto her scalp. She played with their five dogs and laughed like a woman who is blessed with tremendous happiness, contentment and unswerving faith in God.

Since my visit with Jan in 1993, she has completed a second college degree, this one in communications, and she is now an on-air announcer for the local radio station. She also studied theology and has been ordained as the children's pastor at Triumphant Life Church.

Most importantly, she loves every minute of her active life with her two boys. Simply put, Jan says, "I'm a new and different person, triumphant because of God's unending love and wisdom."

After my visit with her I was a new and different person, too. I learned to praise God for everything in my life that makes me new and different, whether it's struggling through one more part-time job to keep my kids in college, learning to be a grandmother for the first time, raising another teenager, or having the courage to end a relationship with a wonderful friend who just wasn't the right one for me.

Jan Turner may not have real flesh-and-blood arms and legs, hands and feet, but that woman has more heart and soul than anyone I ever met before or since. She taught me to grab on to every new and different thing that comes into my life with all the gusto I can muster . . . and just put one foot in front of the other until I get the job done.

Life's Too Short
to Get Breast Cancer

THURSDAY. I'm embarrassed that I've waited four years since my last mammogram. I've heard all the statistics and I know better. But I'm so healthy. I exercise and eat right, and I don't know anyone in my family who ever had breast cancer.

After she takes the X-rays, Alice, the mammography technician, asks me to have a seat on the sofa in the breast exam room while she checks to be sure the quality of the films is okay. I pick up a magazine from the dozen or so spread out on the coffee table and the first article I see is titled "Health Hazard, Confronting My Fear of Breast Cancer."

A few minutes later Alice tells me the films are fine and that I can go. I go home, back to my happy, practically stress-free life.

Friday. 5:00 PM. The phone rings.

"Is this Patricia Lorenz?"

"Yes."

"I'm calling from the radiology department at St. Luke's Hospital. I hate to tell you this so late on a Friday just before the weekend, but the radiologist found a mass in both of your breasts and we need to have you come back for another mammogram and an ultrasound."

"Oh."

"Don't be upset. Ninety-five percent of these are nothing . . . muscle masses or benign lumps or whatever. Nothing to worry about. But I'm also sorry to tell you that we can't work you into the schedule until next Thursday at one thirty."

I answer glibly, "No problem. I'm not worried. No one in my family has had breast cancer, and I breast-fed all four of my children. That's supposed to be good, right? So I'm okay. Next Thursday's fine." *I'm talking too fast and I'm blabbering*, I think to myself.

"Do you have any questions?"

"Yes, how big are these masses?"

"One centimeter in the left breast and about half that in the right."

"Thank you. I'll be there Thursday."

I hang up the phone and resume work at my computer.

Twenty minutes later I realize I'm not working. My mind is racing. A mass in *both* breasts? If it is a mistake, like a shadow or a muscle lump or whatever, wouldn't that just happen in one breast? But *both* breasts? What are the chances of that happening? This must be something.

Saturday. I get up at 5:30 AM. to take my son to school in time to catch the bus for a music contest at another high school. Andrew says I don't need to go because I've already heard all the songs before. I think to myself, *There are so many songs I haven't heard. Will I get to hear enough of them before I die?*

Die? No, I will not think of dying. Andrew's father died when Andrew was nine years old and, no, I am *not* going to die of breast cancer and leave him without any parents. Andrew needs me. I need him. I tell myself to stop this ridiculous thinking.

I resume work at my computer. My long-term goal is to have a draft finished by the end of the month. Today I decide that I will have it finished before the end of next week, the day I go in for the second mammogram and the ultrasound. I write sixteen pages by nightfall, figuring that if I work nonstop all these silly thoughts about breast cancer won't invade my mind. *I am too smart and too sensible to give in to needless worry,* I tell myself.

In bed that night, after eleven o'clock, I worry, think, analyze, ponder, contemplate my will, and decide not to tell my dad and stepmom when I call them tomorrow on Mother's Day.

Sunday. Absolutely the first thought in my head the instant my eyes open in the morning is about this mammogram thing. The small masses in my breasts are filling my mind like a huge evil giant. I sit up quickly and force a smile because the sun is actually out for the first time in days.

Does breast cancer hurt? I wonder. *Or is it just there growing painlessly, insidiously every day?*

All three of my grown children call me long distance for Mother's Day. In spite of my resolve not to tell them, I do. We talk calmly. They don't know how to react. Except for my middle daughter Julia, whose bachelor of science is in health promotion and wellness. She reminds me that she's a certified breast health educator.

She calls me back later after finding all her information

from a conference she attended sponsored by the Wisconsin Women's Cancer Control Program.

"How many women get breast cancer?" I ask.

"One out of eight. But that's women of all ages. Women over fifty have a much higher rate."

Oh great, I think, upset for the first time that I've just turned fifty. Until now, I liked the fact that I was a bundle-of-energy, red-hot, roller-skating mama happily bouncing into her second fifty years. Lately I've been so cocky about my good health that I've told dozens of people that I plan to live to be 120 and that I'll still be roller skating outdoors at eighty. Now I wonder.

"How many women die of breast cancer, Julia?" I ask my knowledgeable daughter.

"One out of four," she says matter-of-factly as she reads from her information on the subject. "It says here that every three minutes a woman is diagnosed with breast cancer and every eleven minutes a woman dies from the disease. Breast cancer is the leading cause of cancer death in women ages forty to forty-nine, but seventy-five percent of breast cancer is diagnosed in women age fifty and older."

The statistics are starting to scare me, so I ask my daughter, "Do you do monthly breast exams, honey?"

"No."

"Julia! You're a professional breast educator and you don't even do them yourself? What's the matter with you?" I realize I'm getting out of control because I have never done regular self-exams either, so I quickly change the subject.

Monday. I take my morning walk and notice with great delight tiny lime-colored leaves bursting out of every branch along the meandering bike path that follows the creek near my home. Do I have fifty or sixty more years on this earth? Or could this be my last springtime? Have I taught my children everything they need to know? Should I make a list of all the things I own and write down which of my children should get what stuff?

Tuesday. My friend Linda calls. She's heard from my friend Sharon about my bad mammogram. After we talk a bit, Linda senses my fear even though I try hard not to let it show.

"Pat, do me a favor and read Psalm 91. Read it carefully and hold it close to your heart and stop worrying . . . completely. When you really trust God, you give up your fear."

I read Psalm 91 (TLB) two or three times. Linda's right. The chapter is very powerful and direct. My favorite verses 1–6 and 9–12 include:

We live within the shadow of the Almighty, sheltered by the God who is above all gods. This I declare, that he alone is my refuge, my place of safety; he is my God, and I am trusting him. For he rescues you from every trap, and protects you from the fatal plague. He will shield you with his wings! . . . His faithful promises are your armor. Now you don't need to be afraid of the dark any more, nor fear the dangers of the day; nor dread the plagues of darkness, nor disasters in the morning. . . . I choose the God above all gods to shelter me. How then can evil overtake me or any plague come near? For he orders his angels to protect you wherever you go. They will steady you with their hands to keep you from stumbling against the rocks on the trail.

Wednesday. Once again, for the fifth day in a row, the first thought in my mind when I wake is about this dastardly mammogram. Even though I wonder what's going to happen tomorrow I notice a calmer feeling. I'm honestly not as worried as I was. Psalm 91 is doing its work.

Later in the day I think about my mother and my grandmother. Mom died at age fifty-seven of amyotrophic lateral sclerosis (Lou Gehrig's disease). Her mother died at age fifty-one, when Mom was only eleven years old, of kidney disease. I wonder, *Would either of them have died of breast cancer if something else hadn't gotten them first?*

Andrew wants to know where he will live if something happens to me. My heart aches at his question, but I matter-of-factly explain that he would live with my brother and his family in Louisville, Kentucky. But I also tell him to stop worrying. Then I tell him about Psalm 91 and say, "I typed it up and laminated it. It's on the kitchen counter." I watch my six-foot-three-inch, sixteen-year-old son read the verses.

Thursday. This is it. The day. The hospital halls, the staff, the routine is all familiar. But this time in the waiting room I actually fall asleep for five or ten minutes until the X-ray technician calls me. I can't believe how relaxed I am.

After five mammograms, much more detailed than the ones last week, during which the technician actually uses a ruler to make sure the specific area where the mass is detected will be visible on the film, I'm told that the radiologist will read the results immediately.

Ten minutes later, the technician returns. "Nothing was detected in the right breast this time, but the left one . . . well, the doctor has ordered an ultrasound for that one because the mass is still visible." And so the technician and I walk down a long hall to the ultrasound room, where this time I lie down on a flat table. This test is completely painless and once again, while the films are being read, I dose off, knowing full well that Psalm 91 has a lot to do with my relaxed, almost catatonic state of mind.

Ten to fifteen minutes later the technician returns. "It's good news. The radiologist is going to advise your doctor that you wait six months and then have another ultrasound to see if there's any change. And, of course, six months after that you must have another mammogram. You need one every year from now on. That's it. You can go."

I smile, thank the woman, although I feel like hugging her, and jump up to get dressed. On the way home I decide to start looking for a pair of good, used in-line skates. It's time to replace my old secondhand roller skates, and if I'm going to be skating when I'm eighty, I need to improve my equipment. After all, the last verse of Psalm 91 (TLB) says, "I will satisfy him with a full life and give him my salvation." I'm certainly up for the *full life* part and will, indeed, accept God's gracious salvation.

Life's Too Short
Not to Let the
Good Times Roll

IN 1989 I ORGANIZED a woman's group called SWILL, which stands for Southeastern Wisconsin Interesting Ladies League . . . women of all ages, all economic backgrounds, different religions, races and lifestyles. SWILL has no dues, no minutes, no committees, no officers, no rules, no dress code, no food worries, no bylaws, no agenda and no purpose. We women simply get together five times a year to talk, laugh and sometimes cry. We sit in a circle and take turns talking, so everyone can hear what everyone else has to say.

One time in 1999 when SWILL met, there were twenty-two women, one of our largest groups ever. The evening was magical in its diversity of life-changing stories. I've changed the names of the SWILL members to protect their privacy, but their stories are true.

Beth described the years of living homeless with her daughter in a car. One night on the interstate when her car broke down, a man stopped. He took Beth and her daughter to a restaurant, fed them and assured them that their lives would change soon. He said a family would help them get on their feet. Then the man simply disappeared. Vanished. Poof. Thin air. Sure enough, a few weeks later a family took Beth and her daughter into their home. That was ten years ago, and today Beth has a good job, a nice apartment and is a remarkable mother to her teenage daughter. Beth still believes in angels.

Annie had just gone through breast cancer surgery and was fearfully facing chemo. We all shed a few tears and many hugs after Annie bravely told her story, which was punctuated by the struggles of her messy divorce, single parenthood, variety of jobs and many moves in recent years.

Grace was beginning an exciting new career as a parish nurse after more than thirty years as an emergency room nurse. In the past year Grace and her retired husband sold the home they'd raised their five children in and moved to a new, smaller home twenty-five miles away. Leaving her old home and neighborhood was traumatic for Grace, but we SWILL members could see courage and excitement spilling out of her soul as she talked about the college courses she was taking to learn to be a parish nurse.

Amy, a beautiful, blonde, forty-something woman who has experienced far too many surgeries and health problems, shared that she had just met a very interesting man, a golfer like her. She giggled and glowed with the joy of a new friendship as she described the fun she was having with her new gentleman.

Peggy, who is a strong leader in her church, shared

that she was seeking a divorce after thirty years of marriage . . . a divorce, she said, that should have happened five years earlier. "These days, my life is a seesaw of loneliness and fear on one hand and excitement and anticipation on the other."

When it was Kelly's turn she said, "As I listen to the ups and downs of what's going on in your lives, I realize how happy and content I am in my life right now. My job is going great, kids are all healthy, my husband and I are getting along fine. I'm working on my master's degree and I love my classes. Hearing your stories makes me want to cherish this moment because I know I'll have worse days and perhaps better days, but for now I'm happy with my life."

Trish, a single parent, shared a similar story. After dreaming for fourteen years about meeting a nice man to date, she has come full circle and finally understands just how happy and full her life is, empty nest and all.

Teresa talked about the emotional breakdown she experienced a few years ago and then described her involvement in a number of volunteer activities including visiting people dying of cancer in a hospice. Teresa demonstrated how giving to others as a volunteer can truly help cure our own ills.

Joan's love of her life, the man she met many years after a painful divorce, had died suddenly nine months before the SWILL meeting. At the previous meeting Joan had cried soulful tears as she shared the story of her three-year romance with her soul mate, stricken suddenly in his fifties by deadly pneumonia. On this night, however, Joan was vibrant, happy and chattering about how she knows she must move forward, meet new people and have some new adventures.

Betty regaled the SWILL gang with an account of a two-week vacation that made *National Lampoon's Family Vacation* look like a picnic at the beach. Natural disasters, transportation problems, a rock slide, and the fact that both she and her hubby were sick much of the trip took their toll. Betty said she fully expected cattle rustlers to hijack the train before they finally arrived home totally exhausted.

I learned a lot about life that night at SWILL. I learned that it's jam-packed with ups and downs and that it often takes a group like SWILL to help us see up close and personal that at any given time, somebody is worse off than we are.

That night, after everyone left, as I put away the cheese spread and dumped the ice cubes, I played a song called "The Bug," sung by Mary Chapin Carpenter. As upbeat and danceable as that song is, the words were haunting. I listened and thought about our SWILL meeting that night, and I understood that it takes a body of friends in one room to help us see that the good often gets better, the bad often gets worse, but more often than not, the average stuff in between is pretty doggone special.